THE CENTRAL AMERICAN REFUGEES

THE CENTRAL AMERICAN REFUGEES

Elizabeth G. Ferris

PRAEGER

New York
Westport, Connecticut
London

Library of Congress Cataloging-in-Publication Data

Ferris, Elizabeth G.
    The Central American refugees.

    1. Refugees—Central America. 2. Central America—
Politics and government—1979– . 3. United States—
Politics and government—1981– . I. Title.
HV640.5.C46F47   1986   362.8'7'08968728   86–21178
ISBN 0-275-92221-9 (alk. paper)

Library of Congress Catalog Card Number: 86-21178
ISBN: 0-275-92221-9

First published in 1987

Praeger Publishers, 521 Fifth Avenue, New York, NY 10175
A division of Greenwood Press, Inc.

Printed in the United States of America

The paper used in this book complies with the
Permanent Paper Standard issued by the National
Information Standards Organization (Z39.48-1984).

10 9   8   7   6   5   4   3   2   1

CONTENTS

1

Comparing National Policies
toward the Central American Refugees

The violence that has plagued Central America since 1978 has displaced an unprecedented number of people. Seeking to escape the turbulence and the insecurity of their communities, over a million Central Americans have fled their communities to other parts of their countries. Many others have left their homelands in search of safety in neighboring countries or in the United States. For the governments that host them, the refugees present serious political, economic, and social problems. At best their presence is tolerated; at worst, they are deported to face an uncertain future back home. Most of the Central American refugees have sought safety in Mexico, Costa Rica, Honduras, and the United States; the governments of these four countries have responded in different ways to the arrival of thousands of Central Americans at their borders. By examining the determinants of refugee policies in these four countries, we can better understand the way in which governments respond to crises and the human consequences of such policy choices.

Refugee movements—though by no means a new phenomenon in human history—are becoming more prevalent and politically more significant in an increasingly interdependent world. Contemporary refugee migrations involve millions of people on all continents and affect political processes in many diverse regimes. In recent years, the Indochinese boatpeople, the Cuban Marielitos, the Afghan refugees, and the Haitians seeking to enter Florida have received considerable media coverage. But beyond the headlines in the U.S. press, the political impact of refugee migrations is even more striking. Most of the world's refugees are currently living in the Third World, where they strain the already limited resources of the governments that host them. For example, the thousands of displaced Lebanese bear witness to the violence that has ravaged that country, and currently twenty-two African countries host refugees. The existence of these refugees reflects the turbulent processes of contemporary political change.

Political scientists have paid relatively little attention to refugee movements, largely interpreting such migrations as marginal to the central processes of international politics. In the great debates over war and peace, refugees are generally seen as the tragic, but politically irrelevant, by-products of the conflict. The analysis in this volume is based on a different premise: that the displacement of large numbers of people because of political violence is both a reflection of and a catalyst for political change, and exploring the political dimensions of refugee migrations is essential for understanding the nature of international relations in the second half of the twentieth century.

The case of the Central American refugees—while it is true that they are the product of unique historical forces—is nevertheless part of this global political dynamic. The focus of the present study is on the determinants of official policy toward refugees—on understanding the ways in which governments arrive at decisions for dealing with the massive migrations now taking place. A focus on the ways in which governments respond to the presence of the refugees is important to both policymakers and scholars seeking to understand the international consequences of politically motivated migrations. The study of national refugee policy provides opportunities for exploring the interaction of policy determinants on both international and domestic levels. As with immigration policy generally, refugee policymaking lies at the juncture of international and domestic politics and is affected by factors on both levels. Thus Mexico's policies toward the Central Americans pouring across its southern border are affected by the nature of its relationship with the Central American governments and with the United States, as well as by domestic economic conditions and bureaucratic in-fighting within the government. The policies that Mexico takes toward the Central American refugees affect both the number and the type of Central Americans who come to the United States. Thus, refugee policies within the region are clearly interdependent.

The present displacement of an estimated two million Central Americans is a new phenomenon in the region, corresponding to a change in the nature of political violence being used. Guerrilla warfare, brutal counterinsurgency campaigns, and the general incorporation of the civilian populations into political conflicts are directly responsible for the growth in the number of refugees. Analysis of the national responses to this violence and the refugees they produce provides insight into the nature of structural changes currently occurring in the region.

Following a brief discussion of the definitional problems invariably attending the study of refugees, the initial chapter of this study addresses the theoretical issues raised by the study of refugees and offers a framework to guide the comprehensive analysis of refugee policymaking. Chapter 2 presents an overview of the Central American refugees themselves in light of the structural changes the refugees reflect. The following four chapters examine the refugee policymaking processes and outcomes for the governments of Mexico, Costa Rica, Honduras, Nicaragua, and the United States. The refugee policies of other governments are briefly discussed in the concluding chapter, which also addresses the larger theoretical issues raised by the study.

THE DEFINITIONAL DILEMMA OF REFUGEES

Although the term "refugee" is used throughout this study as a convenient shorthand for all of those individuals who have left their countries of origin because of the violence there (violence either personally or generally experienced), these individuals are generally *not* recognized as refugees by the governments that host them. The issue of the status of the Central Americans displaced by violence is an exceedingly controversial one, one that illustrates the general dilemma the whole problem poses for international law.

Refugees have been defined in different ways at different points in human history. For most of recorded history, the expectation was that people living in conquered territory would come under the rule of the victor. While there have always been individuals fleeing political persecution, the development of national boundaries, especially in the post-World War II era, has greatly increased the political significance of such movements.

Since World War II, the principal legal definition of refugees has been that incorporated into the 1951 United Nations Convention Relating to the Status of Refugees and its 1967 Protocol, which extended the convention's provisions to current refugees. This definition of refugees was designed to meet the needs of individuals fleeing persecution in the postwar era. Although conditions have changed since this definition was developed, the UN definition remains the single most widely used formulation for determining refugee status today. The Convention defines as a refugee:

> ... any person who, owing to a well-founded fear of being persecuted for reasons of race, religion, nationality, membership of a particular social group or political opinion, is outside the country of his nationality and is unable or,

owing to such fear, is unwilling to avail himself of the protection of that country, or who, not having a nationality and being outside the country of his former habitual residence, is unable or, owing to such fear, is unwilling to return to it.

Furthermore, the UN Convention provides a set of rights for refugees, including the right of *non-refoulement*—that is, the right not to be forcibly repatriated to the country of origin.

Today, 93 countries have ratified either the 1951 Convention or the 1967 protocol and the UN definition of refugee has been incorporated into many nations' laws, including those of the United States and Canada. However, many other countries hosting large numbers of Central American refugees—for example, Honduras, Guatemala, and Mexico—have not ratified the conventions. Moreover, simply acceding to the conventions is not sufficient to resolve the problem of defining refugees. Finally, the definition itself has serious shortcomings.

The definition excludes those individuals who are displaced by violence or warfare and who have not been singled out for individual persecution. Most of the world's wars (and most of the world's refugees) are found in the Third World, where counterinsurgency campaigns displace whole communities and where casualties among noncombatants are high. But these displaced individuals are not considered refugees under the United Nations definition.

Furthermore, the UN definition excludes those individuals who have been displaced or persecuted because of the violence, but who, for one reason or another, have not left their country of origin. Thus, in El Salvador today, over one million Salvadorans (out of a population of 4.5 million) have left their home communities, but approximately half of those individuals remain within El Salvador. In Guatemala, the national Bishops' Association estimates that one million Guatemalans have been internally displaced by the violence in that country. These individuals are not entitled to either the legal guarantees or to the economic protection offered under the auspices of the United Nations High Commissioner for Refugees (UNHCR). As they cannot prove that they have been individually singled out for persecution, their claims of refugee status are not upheld. The U.S. government, for example, has consistently refused to grant refugee or asylum status to Salvadorans or Guatemalans fleeing the violence of their countries, arguing that a generalized condition of warfare is insufficient grounds for the granting of refugee status. As Elliott Abrams, the Assistant Secretary of State for Human Rights and Humanitarian Affairs, stated "The key to the concept of asylum is targeting. It's not sufficient to note that the country [an applicant comes from] is repressive, violent, or poor. You must show something about you as an individual that would make you a target of persecution—your religion, your race, or something."[1] This interpretation has been challenged in the U.S. courts. In December 1984, the Ninth U.S. Circuit Court of Appeals ruled that a Salvadoran immigrant's neutrality in his country's civil war constitutes a "political opinion" and is therefore a valid basis for asylum. Even with this and other challenges, however, the emphasis in determination of refugee status remains an individual's political beliefs.[2]

While the UN definition seeks to provide a universal definition of refugee status to be applied by all governments at all times, in fact, most definitions are political. It is governments that decide whether an individual—or a group—meets the criteria established by national and international law. And as it is national governments that actually implement the laws, political considerations invariably affect governmental decisions. As A. Suhrke points out, politicized definitions have the advantage that governments can regulate the number of refugees quite easily with little pretense of an equitable refugee policy.[3] Paradoxically, while more states have acceded to the UN convention, more restrictive criteria for refugee admissions have been developed by national governments throughout the world.

Governments subscribing to the UN definition use political persecution as the principal criterion for granting refugee status. Individuals leaving their homelands for economic reasons are not considered refugees. This exclusion of "economic refugees" from the UN and other national definitions of refugee status is a topic of hot debate. While economically-motivated migrants may be as needy as those fleeing political persecution, they are not usually given the same treatment as refugees. The problem of deciding whom to treat as refugees is a difficult one facing all governments confronted with large numbers of individuals wishing to immigrate for diverse reasons. As governments increasingly use economic means as tools of warfare, the distinction between political and economic motivations for flight breaks down.

In this study the term "refugees" is considered to apply to those victims of political violence who seek refuge outside their nation's borders. This definition includes individuals persecuted for their political or religious beliefs, for their ethnic or racial background, and those individuals forced to flee their homelands because of war or terror, whether or not they are singled out for persecution.

Governmental responses to refugees seeking protection encompass a range of actions: decisions on the legal status of those seeking refuge, limits on the numbers of individuals given such legal recognition, policies of settlement (or resettlement elsewhere), financial support given to the refugees, and, in a more general sense, attitudes of encouragement or discouragement to those refugees who have arrived in the country. This study is primarily concerned with the governmental responses of countries of first asylum. Although it may well be in the best interests of all parties concerned to encourage the resettlement of refugees within their general region of origin—Southeast Asians in Southeast Asia, for example, rather than in the United States—the overall policy and logistics necessary to support such regional solutions are not the principal focus of this study. Rather, national policies toward refugees are defined as those governmental actions taken with respect to politically-motivated migrants seeking entry and protection. While this study is based on the assumption that humane and effective refugee policies are those that a) extend both legal and political guarantees to the refugees, b) provide basic levels of subsistence to the refugees, and c) move toward just, "durable solutions" (that is, integration, voluntary repatriation, or resettlement), there are obvious political difficulties with such policies. Most importantly, such policies may serve as a magnet, encouraging the migration of other would-be refugees to the borders of the generous country.[4] Thus governments with generous policies may find themselves "penalized" for their policies of welcome. The case of the Central American refugees provides an interesting opportunity for comparison, as the current political crisis has produced a sudden and (for Latin America) unprecedented wave of migrants who have sought asylum within the region. The variety of Central American refugees who have fled their home countries and the diverse political regimes of the countries that receive them make the comparison of national policies toward the Central American refugees a useful opportunity for studying the determinants of refugee policies.

In comparing the policies of the host governments toward the Central American refugees, we will consider national traditions of political asylum, the foreign policy orientations of the host government, domestic economic conditions, and the relative numbers of refugees arriving in the country. These four factors are expected to be the principal determinants of national policies toward the Central American refugees. Governmental foreign policy orientations are expected to be the most important determinant of refugee policies. Refugee policies, lying as they do at the juncture of domestic and international politics, are particularly susceptible to being used as tools of foreign policy. In spite of international norms providing for humanitarian and apolitical treatment of refugees, refugee policies are inevitably politicized in that they always affect relations between the governments of the sending and the receiving countries. By accepting refugees from a neighboring country, for example, the government is sending a clear message that it accepts the refugees' claims of political persecution. If relations between the governments are good, the refugees are less likely to be believed and accepted. In fact, governments will be more likely to accept as refugees those coming from countries deemed hostile by the host government. As one U.S. State Department official graphically explained, "of course, refugee policy is politicized. We accept as refugees those individuals coming from our 'enemies of the day.' Those coming from friendly countries are simply not accepted as refugees."[5] And until the passage of the 1980 Refugee Act, such a distinction was formally incorporated into U.S. law. Examining the political components of refugee policymaking is thus essential for comparing the refugee policies of governments hosting large numbers of Central American refugees. Before doing that, however, it is important to place the discussion of the Central American refugees into the context of current political conditions in Central America and the massive internal displacements of population that have occurred. Refugees are created by political events and the resolution of refugee situations requires resolution of those events, that is, requires political change.

2

The Context of the
Central American Refugee Crisis

The current flood of Central American refugees fleeing the violent conditions in their countries has occurred in the context of long-established patterns of Latin American migration, strong regional traditions of political asylum, and dramatic changes in the nature of political violence in the region. Those changes in the conduct of revolutionary struggle and especially in governmental responses to attempts to change the system have challenged regional traditions of political asylum. This chapter places the phenomenon of Central American refugee flows into the context of Latin American migration patterns, traditions of political asylum, and contemporary political developments in the refugee-producing countries. The chapter concludes with an examination of the principal characteristics of the Central American refugees themselves.

LATIN AMERICAN MIGRATION PATTERNS

The best known migration patterns in the hemisphere are, of course, from Central America and Mexico to the United States. While Mexico is the most widely publicized source of many undocumented workers in the United States, citizens of other countries, particularly Salvadorans, have long come to the United States in search of economic opportunity. In one of the few studies to examine Central American migration patterns to the United States, Guy Poitras studied samples of Costa Rican and Salvadoran migrants coming to the United States. He found that the migration was largely temporary, with Central American migrants staying an average of two years in the United States and Salvadorans an average of one and a half years. The migrants were overwhelmingly male (75 percent of the Costa Rican sample, 85 percent of the Salvadorans), from urban areas, and represented a relatively differentiated, mobile group of individuals. Far from being the poorest of the poor, the migrants had substantial education, averaging over ten years of formal schooling for both the Salvadoran and Costa Rican migrants. There were significant differences between the Salvadoran and Costa Rican groups in terms of the way in which they entered the United States. Of the Costa Ricans who came to the U.S., 80 percent did so with some kind of official document (most commonly a tourist card), while 40 percent of the Salvadorans used the more costly and dangerous alternative of traveling illegally through Mexico and entering the United States without papers. Most of the migrants did not wish to stay in the United States, although 55-60 percent of both the Salvadorans and the Costa Ricans believed that they would definitely return to the United States to work.[1] The existence of historic patterns of substantial economic migration from Central America to the United States has had a profound impact on the nature of the later, politically-motivated flows of refugees. Established patterns of transportation and large Central American communities in the United States have made the U.S. a very attractive destination for Central Americans seeking protection from domestic turmoil. It has also, however, contributed to a negative backlash among sectors of the U.S. population toward the refugees—particularly within those components of the U.S. government charged with controlling the flow of economic migrants to the United States.

Within the region, Central American borders have been relatively open to migration from neighboring countries. Traditionally, for example, thousands of Guatemalans have come to southern Mexico every year to work in the coffee harvest. Mexican agriculturists depend on this labor and governmental authorities have regularized the immigration process for the temporary workers. Moreover, national borders may artificially divide indigenous groups into citizens of separate nation-states. In patterns similar to those found throughout the Third World, the establishment of national boundaries in nineteenth century Central America often ignored patterns of indigenous settlements. Thus, the Mexican/Guatemalan border runs through indigenous Mayan communities. While some of the Indians are Mexican citizens and others are Guatemalan, there is a deep reservoir of loyalty to the indigenous community itself. The Miskitus—currently a source of considerable controversy—have their traditional homelands in both Eastern Honduras and Nicaragua. The area known as Mosquitia was artificially divided by the colonial authorities in creating the two states.

While Central American borders have historically been relatively fluid, with substantial migration for employment and family reasons, the borders have also been a source of serious tension between the governments. All of the governments of Central America and Mexico have had difficulties with neighboring countries over questions of delimiting the border. Tension has been particularly acute between Mexico and Guatemala. In 1821, the state of Chiapas declared its independence from Spain and both Mexico and Guatemala sought to incorporate the state into their respective national territories. But in 1824 a plebiscite resulted in Mexico's annexation of Chiapas. However, the issue was not settled until 1841 when the remaining territory of Soconusco was formally incorporated into Chiapas. Even after the border treaty was signed in 1895, Guatemalan resentment continued. The issue of the Soconusco region has remained a minor irritant in Guatemalan/Mexican relations throughout the twentieth century, occasionally erupting into open conflict. Thus, in December 1958, Guatemalan air force planes attacked five Mexican fishing boats in Mexican territorial waters, killing three Mexicans and wounding 16 others. Three weeks later Mexican president Adolfo López Mateos announced that diplomatic relations with Guatemala had been severed. In later negotiations, Guatemala asserted that the Mexican fishing boats had been inside Guatemala's historic borders, in other words, off the coast of Chiapas. The incident finally ended with Guatemalan apologies, payment of damages, and resumption of diplomatic relations in September 1959.[2] But while the incident was formally resolved, lingering hostilities continue. As will be discussed in the following chapter, one of the reasons why the issue of Guatemalan refugees in Mexico has been so important is precisely because of constant tension over the issue of the border.

The Guatemalan/Mexican border disputes are paralleled throughout the region. For example, the Costa Rican/Nicaraguan border has been the subject of intense conflict and protracted negotiations between the two governments since both countries became independent in the 1820s. These border conflicts contribute to lingering distrust and suspicion between citizens of the two countries even while there is substantial migration between them for economic and family reasons. The existence of these border disputes automatically converts refugee issues into subjects of national security and of national pride and sovereignty.

Of course the best-known border dispute in Central America was the 1969 war between El Salvador and Honduras. Although the causes of the war were complex, the precipitating factor was continued high migration from El Salvador to Honduras—even when the Honduran economy could no longer absorb the migrants. Given the tremendous difference in population density between El Salvador and Honduras, it is perhaps inevitable that thousands of densely-settled, landless Salvadorans have sought economic security—both jobs and land—in neighboring and relatively sparsely settled Honduras. Indeed by the late 1960s, close to 300,000 Salvadorans—1 in 8 Salvadoran citizens—were living in Honduras. Differences in land tenure patterns made Honduras a much more open society than El Salvador, where oligarchic control of the land resulted in rigid inequality. In El Salvador, the growth of agroexport business resulted in more and earlier pressure on the land than in Honduras. Thus, while Salvadoran sugar exports increased by over 1,000 percent in the 1960s, Salvadorans ranked among the world's five most malnourished peoples.[3] But while Salvadoran migration to Honduras created a sort of safety valve for the Salvadoran government, the migrants placed considerable pressure on Honduran society. In June 1969, in response to both growing economic pressure and political opposition to the Salvadoran presence, the Honduran authorities began expelling Salvadoran immigrants. A new Honduran land reform law was decreed that prohibited Salvadorans from owning land. In July of that year, after a disputed soccer match between El Salvador and Honduras, the Honduran government immediately expelled all Salvadorans and war broke out between the two countries. While the war lasted less than a week, several thousand people on both sides were killed, and 100,000 were left homeless.[4]

The consequences of the soccer war were far-reaching. The Central American Common Market, which had enjoyed a surprising measure of success (at least as measured by traditional economic criteria), was left in shambles. The Honduran military was humiliated because of its poor showing in the war; out of that humiliation came a desire to upgrade Honduran military forces and to salvage national honor vis à vis El Salvador. The expulsion of the Salvadorans greatly increased both the economic misery of El Salvador's poor and the political pressure on the government to respond to the increased population pressure. Moreover, the Honduran/Salvadoran border became a highly controversial issue. Animosity between Salvadoran and Honduran military forces has been somewhat mitigated by political changes in both countries, giving rise to a perception that the two armed forces face a common enemy in the revolutionary movements. As will be discussed much more extensively in the chapter on Honduran policies toward the Salvadoran refugees, the flight of 20,000 Salvadorans into Honduras complicated already difficult relations between the two countries and created pressures to resolve the long-standing border dispute.

POLITICAL MIGRATION

While intra-regional migration for economic purposes has accelerated in the postwar period, Latin America also has a much longer tradition of responding to the needs of political dissidents. Between 1889 and 1954, Latin American countries signed six agreements specifying the rights and obligations of political asylum. Indeed, Latin American governments pioneered the development of the concept of diplomatic asylum. Territorial asylum refers to the right of states to admit individuals to its territory, to allow them to stay there, to refuse to expel or extradite them, and not to prosecute, punish, or otherwise restrict their liberty. The concept of extra-territorial asylum, particularly diplomatic asylum, refers to protection from pursuit granted by a state outside of its territory (that is, in a diplomatic mission, warship, military aircraft, and so forth). While outside of Latin America it is generally conceded that in normal circumstances a state cannot grant asylum in its embassy in a foreign state if the territorial state protests and demands the surrender of the person concerned, in Latin America, the situation is very different. It has become an accepted practice of states to allow other Latin American governments to grant asylum in embassies and a system of granting safe-conduct has been developed for people to leave the country. Various international conferences have regulated this, and in fact, the state giving diplomatic exile does not have to extend territorial asylum unless no other country will accept the exile.[5] Thus, Latin American governments have made a unique contribution to the development of legal principles guiding the treatment of political dissidents. Not only do all Latin American governments subscribe to the Universal Declaration of Human Rights, which proclaims that "everyone has the right to seek and enjoy in other countries asylum from persecution," but the Inter-American Declaration of the Rights and Duties of Man of 1948 (which preceded the Universal Declaration by a few months) also proclaims in Article 27 that "every person has the right in case of pursuit not resulting from ordinary crimes, to seek and receive asylum in foreign territory, in accord with the laws of each country and with international agreements."[6]

Latin American governments have frequently extended political asylum to both political dissidents and to political leaders (ousted by military coups) from other Latin American countries. This legal-diplomatic structure corresponds quite nicely with historic patterns of political violence in Latin America. Prior to World War II, much of Latin America's political violence consisted of military coups in which a few ruling elites were displaced. These individuals sought protection from incoming governments by appealing to other governments for asylum; and in fact, it was in the self-interest of Latin American governments to extend political asylum to individuals displaced from their positions by political violence. Governments granting asylum in such cases might well find themselves seeking diplomatic protection in the future.

While these traditions of asylum were intended for individuals fleeing their governments, there have also always been cases of mass international displacement of individuals in the aftermath of more far-reaching political violence. Thus, during 1910–1923, thousands of Mexicans fleeing the violence of the Mexican revolution sought protection in the United States. By the time of the 1973 Chilean coup, some 18,000 Latin American exiles were living in Chile and had to be resettled in the aftermath of the military *golpe*. Estimates of the number of Chileans forced into exile "begin at 100,000."[7] In addition, at least 500,000 Uruguayans are currently in exile for various reasons, and over the years, about half of Paraguay's population has left for political as well as economic reasons. The 1976 military coup in Argentina endangered many of the 300,000 Latin American exiles living there and added to an already significant Argentine exile population—consisting of some 500,000 Argentine nationals. Indeed by 1983, Perez Esquivel estimated that some two and a half million Argentines had left their country.[8] The largest population of South American political exiles presently resides in Brazil, the majority with no legal status.[9] Throughout the continent, the situation for dissidents and for refugees has changed. While the Southern Cone nations used to provide sanctuary to political dissidents, by the 1970s, they had become refugee-producers.

Within Latin America, certain nations have stood out for their willingness to accept political dissidents. As will be discussed later, both Costa Rica and Mexico have long traditions of accepting exiles. Venezuela has also been a haven for Latin American refugees since 1958, including 30,000 Chileans in the aftermath of the 1973 coup. In fact, in 1978, Venezuela took a number of Portuguese former residents of Mozambique and Angola as well as 132 Nicaraguan political asylees and 200 former political prisoners from Cuba.[10]

Although Latin America has a well-developed tradition of political asylum, this tradition has been unable to meet fully the needs created by the current massive outpouring of Central American refugees.

VIOLENCE IN CENTRAL AMERICA

The present period of expanded violence in Central America dates from the late 1970s with the development of a full-scale revolutionary movement in Nicaragua. But the roots of the violence are much deeper and extend to the core of Central American societies themselves. While the phenomenon of masses of individuals fleeing their homelands is new in Central America, the violence that has produced these refugees is as old as the countries themselves. With few exceptions, the Central American political game has been characterized by the dominance of a wealthy landed elite governing, occasionally with democratic facades and almost always with the active collaboration of the military. After the successful Cuban revolution there were some modest efforts at reform in Central America, but much more successful were the efforts on the part of the ruling elites to cast themselves as the staunch anti-communist allies of the United States. The Central American leaders quickly learned that the way to win Washington's support in putting down opposition movements was to label the opposition as communist. The Central American political game was characterized by the concentration of wealth in the hands of a few, the almost total exclusion of indigenous groups from the political processes, and frequently brutal efforts to prevent the formation of broad-based opposition groups.

Economically, the Central American nations were dependent on the United States; to varying degrees they successfully encouraged the development of indigenous industry and invested heavily in the agro-export sector. While politics seemed stable throughout the 1960s, there were many precipitants of change occurring below the surface. The radicalization of many of Central America's clergy, the formation of mass popular organizations—in spite of the efforts by government to stop them—and the growing disillusionment with the rhetoric of reform created a climate of receptivity to revolutionary alternatives throughout the region.

The Nicaraguan insurrection in 1979 broke the pattern of traditional politics in Central America forever. The revolution's success was made possible by a combination of unique factors—particularly the alienation of the middle and industrial classes by President Anastasio Somoza's greed in the aftermath of the 1972 earthquake, and the early, spectacular successes of the Sandinistas, which embarrassed the government and inspired the opposition. Prodded by Jimmy Carter's human rights policy, the Somoza regime attempted modest reforms through sporadic openings to the moderate opposition—reforms interspersed with increased repression. In a cycle to be repeated in El Salvador and Guatemala, governmental repression was extended to peasant populations accused of harboring guerrillas. The repression radicalized the peasant populations, which in turn led to even more brutal repression, triggering the cycle once again.[11]

In Central America, both governments and revolutionary movements have learned from the successful Nicaraguan insurgency that the countryside is the key to revolution. Guerrilla forces have concentrated their efforts on the peasantry, and the governments of El Salvador and Guatemala have extended their operations to rural areas. Counterinsurgency campaigns designed to intimidate rural populations from aiding the guerrillas have produced casualties far higher than ever before in Central America's turbulent history. Guerrilla retaliation against government sympathizers coupled with the far more common violence of rightwing paramilitary forces has created a climate of fear and terror throughout El Salvador and Guatemala.

As discussed below, the political situation in these two countries is becoming increasingly polarized; moderate leaders of popular organizations and of centrist political movements have been killed, forced underground, or have fled into exile abroad. As casualties mount and as revolutionary violence continues to escalate in rural areas, governments of both countries have turned to Vietnam War-style "pacification" techniques. Increased military operations in the rural areas, "scorched earth" policies, and the development of "protected villages" (à la Vietnam's "strategic hamlets") have led to widespread intimidation of peasants in the region. Moreover, governmental definitions of the enemy have broadened; the enemy is presently considered to be those individuals who are not actively supporting the government. So in both El Salvador and Guatemala the governments have created "civilian patrols" to keep the peace in local communities and at the same time serve as a check on the loyalty of peasant populations.

The difficulties of the new Nicaraguan government in consolidating their revolution have been exhaustively analyzed elsewhere.[12] Certainly the leaders made many political mistakes; governmental policies toward the Nicaraguan indigenous groups, as discussed below, have created many political problems for the government. The economic difficulties of the regime coupled with the escalating war along both national borders have greatly damaged the government's ability to rule effectively. But clearly most of the economic difficulties the Sandinista regime has had to face are due to U.S. government funding for the so-called *contras,* which has kept Nicaragua in a permanent state of war and has caused an extraordinarily high economic and human cost. Over 4,000 Nicaraguans have been killed in the war with the *contras.* Moreover, the diversion of scarce economic resources away from meeting the revolution's objectives has been very damaging to public morale. The economic pressures brought to bear by the U.S. government on Nicaragua have taken a high toll. Economic scarcity is a fact of life. While the Nicaraguan government struggles for its very survival, conditions throughout Central America have deteriorated.

The war in Central America, coupled with economic pressures common throughout the Third World, have produced serious economic problems for the governments of the region. The violence in El Salvador and Guatemala has sharply diminished both agricultural and industrial pro-

Table 2.1: Central American Economic and Social Indicators, 1980

Country	Population (1,000s)	Percent Urban	Land Area 1,000 sq. km	Density[1]	GNP (Millions $)	GNP per Capita	Literacy Rate	Percent School-aged Children in School	Life Expectancy	Infant Mortality Rate[2]	Percent of Population with Safe Water
Costa Rica	2,404	43	51	47	4,622	$1,923	93	55	70	24	81
El Salvador	4,718	41	21	225	3,420	725	65	47	62	53	48
Guatemala	7,120	39	215	4	556	1,096	50	33	59	72	42
Honduras	3,816	36	112	34	2,414	633	60	48	58	90	55
Nicaragua	2,497	53	130	19	2,090	837	66	54	56	90	46
Mexico	70,111	67	1,973	36	181,611	2,590	83	69	65	60	59

[1]Population per square kilometer of area.

[2]Deaths under one year of age per 1,000 live births.

Source: Ruth Leger Sivard, *World Military and Social Expenditures* (Washington, D.C.: World Priorities, 1983).

duction in these countries. Declining production, growing unemployment, and the climate of uncertainty has limited growth and investment, causing even further hardship on the people. Tables 2.1 and 2.2 present a summary of present economic, political, and social characteristics of the Central American nations.

TABLE 2.2: Land and Poverty in Central America

Country	Percent of Farmland Controlled by Largest Landowners	Percent Landless	Percent In Absolute Poverty[a]	Percent of Children Under 5 Malnourished 1976
Costa Rica	1% control 36% of farmland	40	40	52
El Salvador	1% control 41% of farmland	60	74	74
Guatemala	1% control 34% of farmland	27	70	83
Honduras	4% control 56% of farmland	35	77	81
Nicaragua[b]	2% control 48% of farmland	32	57	69

[a]"Absolute Poverty" is defined as being unable to afford a minimum recommended diet.

[b]Nicaragua figures are pre-Revolution.

Source: Latin-American Hemispheric Education, *Resources Center Bulletin,* 2, No. 1 (Spring 1985), 2.

The desperate poverty and growing inequality in Central America are obvious throughout the region. Less than 1 percent of the region's farms occupy 40 percent of the available farmland. The poorest 20 percent of the population receives only 3 percent of the national income. Per capita income figures obscure the grim reality of most rural families. In Guatemala, El Salvador, and Honduras, 80 percent of rural families do not earn enough to purchase basic necessities while 50 percent live in extreme poverty, unable even to buy the food necessary for survival.[13] Hostilities between neighboring countries, particularly between Nicaragua and Honduras, have disrupted regional commercial relations. The Central American Common Market—once heralded as an example of the benefits of regional cooperation—never fully recovered from the 1969 war between El Salvador and Honduras and is now in shambles. The fall in prices of some of Central America's principal exports (particularly coffee) and continued high prices for oil-based products, have sharply limited governmental revenues and have contributed to balance of payments difficulties. International debt crises in Costa Rica, Honduras, and Mexico have increased political pressures on those governments—pressures to resolve national economic difficulties that are reflected in more conservative governments and more protectionist measures. The debt burdens are particularly acute in Honduras (47 percent of the GNP), Costa Rica (80 percent) and Nicaragua (93 percent), while the situation in El Salvador has been somewhat alleviated by the tremendous U.S. economic aid to that country.[14] The economic difficulties have contributed to the instability and to the political difficulties giving rise to refugee flows. At the same time, the economic troubles in all the countries of the region have limited the governments' policy options toward the refugees. In studies of migration throughout the world, it is almost a foregone conclusion that when economic conditions are poor, national hospitality to foreigners declines.

The growing internationalization of the Central American conflict has also affected the flow of refugees and governmental policies toward the refugees. What began as largely domestic revolutionary efforts in Nicaragua, El Salvador, and Guatemala have been transformed into an issue of East/West confrontation. A rapid increase in U.S. economic and military aid to the beleaguered countries of the region (Table 2.3), together with an expanding U.S. military presence has increased the international stakes of the region's conflict. U.S. aid to the region has skyrocketed. In FY 1979, U.S. military loans to El Salvador totalled only $4,000. The next year, President Carter increased that figure to $6 million.[15] Bellicose U.S. policies toward Nicaragua—including verbal threats, economic sanctions, and military efforts to overthrow the government— have further increased tensions in the region. The presence of U.S. military advisers, bases, and training programs together with the militarization of border areas through Central America have given the issue of the refugees a strategic and military dimension that affects governmental responses to their plight.

Table 2.3: U.S. Military/Economic Aid to Central America (in millions of dollars)

Country	FY 1981	FY 1982	FY 1983	FY 1984	FY 1986 (Proposed)
Costa Rica	0.0/15.2	2.1/51.7	4.6/214.2	72.2/36.2	3/187
El Salvador	35.5/114.0	82.0/182.2	81.3/245.6	331.5/75.4	351/133
Guatemala	0.0/19.0	0.0/15.5	0.0/29.6	50.4/26.6	10/77
Honduras	8.9/36.4	31.3/80.6	48.3/106.0	134/46.2	143/88

Source: "Aid and U.S. interests in Latin America and the Caribbean" *Current Policy* 66 (March 5, 1985) and Richard Alan White, *The Morass: United States Intervention in Central America* (New York: Harper and Row, 1984), 236-37.

While this discussion has emphasized the common denominators of political and economic life in Central America, it has obscured some important differences between countries. As will be discussed later in the chapters on national refugee policies, specific national characteristics—such as Costa Rica's democracy, and Honduran patterns of land tenure—have contributed to different responses to the refugees. Similarly, the violence in Guatemala and El Salvador has taken different forms and resulted in different patterns of refugee migrations.

This analysis now turns to an examination of the causes of the refugee flows in Central America. It is in the discussion of the causes, particularly the root causes, of refugee migrations that the study of refugees becomes intensely political. In fact, the UNHCR has stayed away from analyses of the causes of refugee migrations precisely because of the realization that their highly political nature could threaten the agency's ability to act. Nonetheless, as J. W. Clay says, to study refugee migrations and to consider alternative solutions to refugee problems is impossible without an understanding of the causes of those refugee movements.[16]

EL SALVADOR

Coffee has been the foundation of El Salvador's economy and of its ruling elite. In 1931, historian David Brown wrote that coffee "produced 95.5% of export earnings, paid the country's taxes, proportioned funds for central and local governments, financed the construction of roads, ports, and railroads, created permanent or seasonal employment, and made the fortunes of a few."[17]

As many authors writing about El Salvador have stressed, coffee and the land to grow it on were central to the creation of a social order based on the domination by a landed oligarchy. A coalition between the owners of the large coffee plantations and the military was based on a tacit agreement not ever to redistribute the land. Efforts to change the system—such as the 1932 peasant uprising—were brutally smashed by those in power. The casualties from that uprising are widely reported as 30,000 deaths and the destruction of indigenous culture. While the oligarchy maintained its tight control into the 1960s, industrialization produced not only economic growth, but tensions within the ruling circle. The formation of the Christian Democratic Party in 1962 reflected divisions between the landed oligarchy and the growing power of the industrialists.

Industrialization, coupled with population growth, led to increased unemployment—and ominously, to an increased number of landless peasants. Cynthia Arnson reports that between 1961 and 1975, the number of landless peasants increased from 11 percent to 40 percent of the rural population.[18] After the 1969 closing of the safety valve of migration to Honduras, conditions in El Salvador worsened. Today over 90 percent of the country's farms are too small to provide enough food for just one family. In the last twenty years, the number of landless rural Salvadorans has increased five times, from 12 percent to 60 percent of the total rural population. The formation of mass popular organizations to protest unjust social structures was paralleled by the rise of "anti-communist" paramilitary groups. The government responded to the "rightwing" death squads with toleration and to the "leftwing" mass organizations with repression. As social conditions worsened and both the government and its opponents were aware of events in neighboring Nicaragua, change began within the military.

In October 1979 a group of somewhat reformist junior officers overthrew the government of General Carlos Humberto Romero. These military officers feared a Nicaraguan-style revolution in El Salvador if reforms were not implemented, and they formed a civilian/military junta to implement basic social reforms. The junta ran into trouble from the very beginning. Power remained in the hands of the traditional military forces and the junta found its efforts at social reform stymied at every turn. Repression continued, the press remained censored, the university stayed closed and most ominously of all, the violence escalated. The death squads operated with impunity. Some have estimated that 1,000 Salvadorans per month were assassinated by the death squads and the government was powerless to stop the violence. On January 3, 1980, the civilian members of the junta resigned and were replaced by Christian Democrats. The participation of leaders of the Christian Democratic Party (PDC) in the junta was rejected by a large segment of the party. Nonetheless PDC leader José Napoleón Duarte emerged as a civilian spokesman for the junta and was viewed by Washington as a moderate alternative to the increase in apparent brutality by the right and the growing political and military strength on the left. Currently Major Roberto d'Aubuisson, leader of the country's most conservative party, ARENA (Nationalist Republican Alliance), has emerged as the spokesman for the right.

Rightwing death squads continued to operate to eliminate "communists" from the country. Indeed, on March 24, 1980, Salvadoran Archbishop Oscar Romero was assassinated by rightwing sharpshooters as he was saying mass. His assassination came the day after he had implored the National Guard to lay down their arms, to respond to a higher law, and to stop the killing. He recognized that the National Guard was not in any way a neutral, professional armed force, but rather an active perpetrator of the violence. In fact, the National Guard and other security forces had become and remain the principal perpetrators of the violence in the country.

Shortly after Romero's murder, the leftist opposition groups joined together in the FDR (Frente Democrático Revolucionario), which has served as the diplomatic representative of the FMLN (Frente Farabundo Martí de la Liberación Nacional). The FMLN was formed in the early 1970s as an effort to direct the armed struggle and is currently composed of several revolutionary groups with diverse ideological orientations (although all consider themselves Marxist to some extent). Estimates of the FMLN's support range from 30 to 80 percent of the Salvadoran population.[19] Currently the guerrillas control between 25 and 35 percent of the nation's territory.

The war has had a serious economic cost. Currently, El Salvador has a foreign debt of $1.2 billion and has been involved in protracted negotiations with the International Monetary Fund. In the last five years, the GDP has dropped 28 percent and wages have lost 65 percent of their purchasing power.[20] Weather, disease, and guerrilla attacks have damaged agricultural exports. Coffee production was expected to fall by 40 percent in 1984. Growing pressure from labor unions adds to Duarte's difficulties. Economic and military aid from the United States became essential to continuing the war effort. As violence escalated in the early 1980s (including the murder of four U.S. churchwomen), U.S. military aid to El Salvador increased.

While Duarte's government announced various reforms, including an agrarian reform, real power lay in the hands of the vastly superior military forces. As a result of U.S. pressure, elections were held in March 1982 for a Constituent Assembly to draw up a new constitution for the country. The left refused to participate in the elections, arguing that unless the safety of the opposition candidates could be guaranteed, elections would be meaningless. In spite of U.S. pressure, Roberto D'Aubuisson was elected president of the National Assembly on a platform of unleashing the security forces on the opposition and dismantling the agrarian reform. However, the United States was able to prevail on the military to accept Alvaro Magaña as the country's provisional president. While Magaña was to provide a facade of democracy, real power remained in the hands of the military. In March 1984 elections for the presidency were held; in spite of widespread criticism of the exclusion of the left from the elections, the U.S. administration heralded the elections as evidence that its massive military aid was in support of a democratic regime. The Duarte victory and subsequent government sought to present an image of a moderate, sincere alternative to the violent forces of left and right.

Yet the violence continues in El Salvador. The Duarte regime, although perhaps truly sincere in its reformist intentions, has been unable to stop the violence. The military continues to hold the upper hand and the death squads operate with impunity. Casualties have reached the 50,000 mark, and virtually all human rights organizations agree that the majority of the victims have been civilian noncombatants. An increase in the air war in the northern part of the country has destroyed villages and farmlands, and killed increasing numbers of individuals and forced many to flee their homes. The government has been unable to alter the military situation substantially; the opposition still controls approximately one third of the national territory. Morale and discipline among Salvadoran soldiers is notably low; the forced conscription of many youths into the military has created an army unwilling to take risks and suspicious of participation in night patrols. In fact, one indication of the failure of the land war in overcoming resistance is the growing emphasis on the air war. The role of the United States in the air war is interesting. While it is the United States that is supplying the equipment for destruction—the planes, bombs, training the pilots—the U.S. government officially denies that there is a problem with the aerial bombing. The Lawyers' Committee for International Human Rights and Americas Watch considered the implications of such a U.S. disavowal for the violence of the air war: "unfortunately [this U.S. support] may encourage the Salvadoran armed forces to continue bombing nongovernment areas with impunity and without regard to the presence of noncombatants."[21]

The violence of the death squads continues; bodies still regularly appear on the sides of Salvadoran highways and the fact that death squad members have not been tried for the violence has created a certainty that their actions are condoned by the military forces. Indeed, many writers maintain that the death squads are largely composed of former and active duty security forces.

The human toll of the violence in El Salvador is overwhelming; 500,000 Salvadorans—ten percent of the country's population—have been forced to leave their communities for other areas of the country. An additional 500,000 to 750,000 have fled El Salvador completely, seeking safe haven outside their national borders. These figures are enormously high. Even at the height of the Vietnam War, only 8 percent of the population was displaced.[22]

The question of Salvadoran refugees in other countries must be understood in the larger context of the thousands of displaced persons who remain in El Salvador. In 1983, the Legal Aid Office of the Archdiocese of San Salvador distinguished three categories of internally displaced persons: 1) family and collaborators of the security and paramilitary forces (15,000) who are evacuated before military operations to government-held areas where they receive aid from the government and the Salvadoran Red Cross; 2) peasants who have fled to San Salvador and are seeking aid from centers run by the Archdiocese (4,000); and 3) peasants living in areas in conflict who seek refuge with other peasants or in church-run institutions (100-400 thousand).[23] Several recent studies of the condition of the displaced persons indicate that the situation of the internally displaced Salvadorans is deplorable. Conditions in the camps are very bad, and the camps are insufficient to hold more than 25 percent of the displaced population. A study trip by two staff members of the U.S. Senate Judiciary Committee noted that the camps in Morazon province were particularly bad. "In physical terms, they are just a cut above the worst refugee camps during the Bangladesh crisis outside Calcutta in 1971 or during the worst days of the Vietnam war."[24] In fact as another observer noted, "[D]isplaced Salvadorans would find much better conditions in virtually any refugee camp or settlement in a nearby country of asylum."[25]

But the problems of internally displaced Salvadorans go far beyond the deplorable physical condition in which they live. The safety of the displaced persons is constantly at risk. The Salvadoran government provides assistance to approximately 262,000 displaced persons who have registered with CONADES, the Salvadoran government agency charged with relief to the displaced persons. The ICRC (International Committee of the Red Cross) provides aid to approximately 80,000 other displaced Salvadorans, most of whom are in guerrilla-controlled zones. Another 125,000 displaced persons in government-controlled areas of El Salvador are outside the scope of relief programs and the ICRC. Twenty religious and secular organizations provide some relief to these 125,000. Caritas, for example, estimates that it serves 50,000 displaced persons while CESAD (Comité Evangélico Salvadoreño de Ayuda y Desarrollo), reported feeding 16,000 people per month.[26] Many of these organizations refuse to accept U.S. government funds, feeling that to do so is to compromise their nonpartisan nature and hence their ability to fulfill their duties to the refugees. This creates political difficulties for some of the relief organizations who are viewed with suspicion by government forces. Many political groups have sought to use the displaced persons for political purposes. S. Dillon reports that it is increasingly difficult for aid to be distributed in a humanitarian fashion as political parties, missionaries, and various political groups all seek to use the refugees for their own purposes.[27] Indeed the four U.S. churchwomen who were killed in 1980 had been working with displaced persons.

Virtually all U.S. aid to the displaced is administered through CONADES and in fact almost the entire Salvadoran budget for displaced persons comes from the Agency for International Development (AID) and the Department of State. The Salvadoran government's inefficiency in distributing the aid has been widely noted.[28]

Many Salvadorans are afraid to register with the government as Salvadoran officials condition receipt of humanitarian aid on government registration forms that require substantial information about an individual's background and family members. Local army commanders must approve the lists of registered displaced persons before requests for aid can be allocated. Thus, displaced Salvadorans must not only fear that this information will be given to local security forces but also retaliation by government forces.

There is good reason for displaced persons to fear government retaliation by security forces. There have been countless incidents of torture, arbitrary arrest, harassment, and murder of displaced persons and relief workers by the security forces.[29] Indeed, many members of the Salvadoran security forces see displaced persons as guerrilla sympathizers. There has been a constant pattern of intimidation of the displaced persons living in camps by Salvadoran security forces. The Lawyers' Committee for International Human Rights and Americas Watch, for example, report that there are virtually no able-bodied adult males in the camps for displaced persons in El Salvador. In fact, the Lutheran-run Fé y Esperanza camp does not even accept young males, in hopes of protecting its residents.[30] Approximately 4,000 displaced Salvadorans live in church compounds as virtual prisoners. The displaced persons are afraid to leave the campgrounds for fear of violence by the military.[31]

The situation of the displaced persons is thus characterized by economic hardship, legal uncertainty, and constant fear. CONADES estimates that 74 percent of the employable displaced population registered with CONADES was unemployed in 1984. Undoubtedly the unemployment rate is higher among the unregistered displaced.[32] In 1983, the Salvadoran military launched a major "return to the village" campaign for displaced persons. This campaign was intended to ease some of the urban congestion caused by the refugees flocking to the cities. It was also designed to secure the countryside from guerrilla attack and infiltration and to restore municipal government and services. According to the U.S. Senate Judiciary Committee investigation, this program has resulted in a "musical chairs" situation where there are substantial movements of people, all seeking to move to more secure areas but reluctant to return to their own homes.[33]

For Salvadoran noncombatants, the threat of violence is very real. The actions of the death squads, the seemingly random brutality of the security forces, the massive aerial bombing of contested areas, and the major economic dislocations produced by the war combine to produce an intolerable situation. By the hundreds and the hundreds of thousands they have fled their country; indeed as the discussion of the situation of the displaced persons has shown, the Salvadoran refugees who leave may be the fortunate ones. Less is known about the situation in neighboring Guatemala. As summarized below, conditions in Guatemala are also becoming increasingly intolerable.

GUATEMALA

As in the case of El Salvador, Guatemala's present political crisis is rooted in a historic pattern of dominance by a landed elite and by close ties with the United States. In fact, the history of Guatemala in this century is the history of the United Fruit Company and close United States/Guatemalan relations. Following decades of rule by the military and the landed aristocracy, and close relations with U.S. business interests, in 1944 a popular coalition managed to elect reformist Juan José Arevalo to the presidency. He and his successor, Jacobo Arbenz, enacted agrarian reform legislation (particularly threatening to the United Fruit Company), labor and educational reforms, and an independent foreign policy line. In 1954, the Arbenz regime was overthrown by CIA-backed Col. Castillo Armas. The message for Guatemala, and for all of Latin America was clear: the U.S. government would oppose— with military force if necessary—efforts by leftist governments to enact radical social change. In fact, U.S. actions in 1954 can be seen as being repeated since 1984 in Nicaragua.

Since the 1954 overthrow, military governments have alternated with fraudulent elections to provide uninterrupted repressive rule in Guatemala. Massive U.S. military and economic aid in the 1960s provided support for an increasingly powerful military force. The rise of popular organizations, the awakening of Catholic movements in support of social change, and the development of mass organizations led to increasing repression on the part of the government. As opposition forces increased in power and scope, the Guatemalan government reacted with more far-reaching programs of repression. Anyone opposing the government was branded as an enemy of the state and subject to reprisals. Then-president Col. Arana stated in the early 1970s "If it is necessary to turn the country into a cemetery in order to pacify it, I will not hesitate to do so."[34]

As in El Salvador, the emergence of death squads and the systematic elimination of any moderate opposition leaders created a climate of widespread fear and terror throughout the country. Amnesty International reported that between 1966 and 1976, 20,000 people died at the hands of the death squads.[35] Numerous international organizations have expressed dismay at the continuing widespread violations of human rights in Guatemala. In December 1984 the United Nations General Assembly voted by 85 to 11 (with 47 abstentions and the negative vote of the United States) to support a resolution condemning the repression in Guatemala. On December 1, 1984, the Archbishop of Guatemala, Monsignor Prospero Penados del Barrio, said "[t]he country is bleeding to death; the violence respects nothing and no one."[36] In fact, the U.S. government stands virtually alone in its efforts to downplay the scale of human rights violations in Guatemala. In its 1983 Human Rights Country Reports, most of the deaths in Guatemala are attributed to military encounters between the government and guerrilla forces although the report does attribute some responsibility to government security forces.[37]

The violence and brutality of the Guatemalan generals finally convinced the Carter administration to distance itself from the Guatemalan government. In 1977 U.S. military sales to Guatemala were suspended as the Guatemalan military defiantly refused to submit to processes of human rights certification. However, the ban on military sales did not prevent the U.S. government from shipping "nonmilitary" goods (such as ammunition, small weapons, trucks, and light aircraft) to Guatemala.

As moderate opposition leaders were systematically eliminated, the guerrilla organizations became widely recognized as the only effective opposition movement. Currently four principal military organizations make up the URNG (Unidad Revolucionaria Nacional de Guatemala): the Guatemalan Workers Party (PGI), Rebel Armed Forces (FAR), Guerrilla Army of the Poor (EGP), and the Revolutionary Organization of the People in Arms (ORPAR). These rebel groups seek to overthrow the current military government, redistribute the wealth and land of the wealthy elite, and establish an independent, autonomous government by the people. In the past few years, the revolutionary forces have sought to incorporate the indigenous masses into the revolution. Some 60 percent of Guatemala's population is officially classified as Indian; for generations the indigenous peasants have been marginal to national political processes, socially isolated from the rest of the population by a far-reaching intensive system of prejudice, and exploited as cheap labor. The ruling elite have fostered enmity between *ladino* and *indio* groups as a way of increasing their own power.

Following elections in 1982 and another military coup, in June 1982, General Efraín Rios Montt seized power from the junta and established himself as sole director. Rios Montt had a long history of involvement in Guatemalan politics although he was unusual in his evangelical devotion to a small California religious sect. He came to power seeing it as his Christian duty to restore order and to triumph over the guerrilla forces. In fact, he saw his government as locked in a struggle between good and evil and emphasized his willingness to fight until death. He ordered the guerrillas to lay down their arms and when they refused, he retaliated with massive violence. Most ominously, campaigns were directed against civilian populations judged guilty of supporting armed revolutionaries. Formation of civilian defense patrols (through forced conscription of peasants) was accompanied by massive relocation programs intended to move indigenous population groups to villages where they could be protected from enemy actions. When peasants were reluctant to abandon their traditional lands, brutal acts of destruction were carried out.

Various governmental programs—"Beans and Bullets," "The Three T's" (Work, Roof, and Food, for the Spanish initials)—have increased the government's penetration of hitherto marginalized populations. While for generations the rural indigenous populations had been excluded from politics, neutrality or indifference is no longer an option for them. By seeking to deny the guerrillas the support of the rural populations, the Guatemalan regime has fundamentally and irreversibly changed the nature of politics in the country. The message to the indigenous groups was very clear: the government was determined to destroy the indigenous communities if they appeared to oppose the government. Some writers suggest that the destruction of the indigenous communities stemmed from both a racist desire to eliminate indigenous culture and from the greed of certain military officers who wanted Indian lands.[38] As the counterinsurgency campaigns heated up, the number of displaced peasants increased. Hundreds of thousands of Guatemalan peasants—particularly indigenous groups—left their home communities in search of safe haven. As in the case of El Salvador, the majority of those displaced by the violence remain within Guatemalan territory. The Guatemalan bishops estimate that one million Guatemalans are internally displaced. The UNHCR's estimate is much lower; yet the UN has not received permission to enter the country to study the plight of the displaced Guatemalans (or of the estimated 70,000 Salvadorans currently seeking sanctuary in Guatemala).

Many of the Guatemalans have made the treacherous journey overland through the Lacondona jungle into Mexico. The Guatemalan government clearly views those who leave their communities as subversives and has sought to prevent their flight. Indeed, the flood of refugees in 1981/82 decreased to a mere trickle; few observers feel that the refugees have stopped coming because the situation has improved. In June 1983 the Comité de Ayuda a Refugiados Guatemaltecos and the Mexican Social Security Administration estimated that at least 8,000 Guatemalans have died trying to reach Mexican territory.[39] Indeed, the few refugees getting through report that the brutality continues unabated. Rather, the

Guatemalan military has militarized the border, creating a situation where to pass through into Mexico has become virtually impossible.

The increasing violence against the indigenous communities and the growing militarization of the border have been made possible by large-scale foreign aid programs. During the time when U.S. military aid to Guatemala was officially suspended, Israel increased its arms exports to Guatemala along with stepped-up training of Guatemalan military officers. In June 1981, the Reagan administration approved a $3.2 million cash sale of military vehicles to Guatemala. In January 1983 the Reagan administration "announced the decision to sell $6 million of helicopter spare parts and communications equipment to the Guatemalan Air Force to service another $25 million of Bell helicopters which have been sold to Guatemala in violation of the arms sales restrictions."[40]

U.S. aid to Guatemala must be understood in the context of that nation's grave economic situation. Guatemala's high external debt has led it to extended negotiations with the IMF, which has suspended its standby credit due to the regime's noncompliance. In 1984, underemployment averaged 40 percent, foreign investment declined precipitously, the tourist industry was at a standstill, and capital flight for 1983 was estimated at $130 million, or 12 percent of total export earnings.[41] The economic cost of the domestic conflict has been very high.

The Guatemalan regime of Rios Montt became increasingly isolated from the other Central American governments—in part because of Guatemalan brutality at home and Rios Montt's apparent willingness to talk with the Nicaraguan Sandinista leadership. Furthermore, Guatemala's historic claim to two thirds of Belize's territory has created serious problems in further cooperation within the region—cooperation that is clearly desired by the U.S. government as a means of confronting growing Sandinista military power. Moreover, Rios Montt had alienated several important Guatemalan military leaders because of his support for Protestant-style Christianity and the visible corruption of his regime. In August 1983 General Oscar Mejía Victores overthrew Rios Montt. Mejía Victores promised to continue Rios Montt's "war to the death" against the guerrillas while working with the leaders of the other Central American nations to contain Sandinista military power. The Reagan administration has responded to the change in administration and orientation in Guatemala with a proposed $10 million in military sales credits and $250,000 in training funds for 1984.

Elections in 1985 led to the victory of Marco Vinicio Cerezo Arevalo. Although lauded by the Reagan administration for the "return to democracy" in Guatemala, in fact it is unlikely that the situation will change dramatically in the near future. The military remains the dominant power in the country and violence against civilian populations continues. In their pastoral letter for the 1985 elections, the Guatemalan Catholic bishops warned that the holding of elections, while certainly a positive step, should not be regarded as a panacea for Guatemala's many problems:

> Certainly the holding of the general elections may be the first step in the attaining of a better situation in Guatemala. But, in order that the longed-for results be obtained, there must be not only freedom at the moment of casting one's vote, but also a whole series of particular social, political, and economic conditions, which are, unfortunately, not happening in Guatemala. In effect there still persist in Guatemala harsh violence, lack of respect for human rights, and the breaking of basic laws. It is a fact that any citizen pressured, terrorized or threatened is not fully able to exercise his/her right to vote or be elected conscientiously. It is not easy to exercise the right to vote when the ideology of national security prevails over the legislation which supports, orients and guarantees the free action of citizens. Hungry, impoverished and desperate people are easy prey to the demagogery which comes to them at election time and are not fully able to discern for whom they should vote with serenity and complete awareness.

President-elect Cerezo indicated during the campaign that he does not intend to alter the fundamental socioeconomic system. Although he has announced several reform measures, the power of the landowners will not be challenged, the settlement of rural Guatemalans into protected villages will continue, and the military will remain as the dominant power in questions of national security. Indeed, it is the military's real veto power over reformist measures that most seriously limits fundamental change in the country.

Meanwhile, of course, the situation of the Guatemalan refugees and displaced persons continues to be serious. While the flow of Guatemalans outside the country has diminished, reports are that the number of internally displaced is increasing.

A third group of refugees in Central America—in addition to the Salvadorans and Guatemalans fleeing their governments' counterinsurgency campaigns—are the Nicaraguans. As discussed in the section below, the Nicaraguan refugees, particularly those from indigenous groups, have become politically important. In fact, their situation is being overtly manipulated by other governments, which is indicative of both the internationalization of Central American conflicts and its consequences on the refugees.

NICARAGUA

The Nicaraguans who have left their country have done so for several reasons: 1) members of indigenous groups such as the Miskitus have fled what they perceive as ethnic persecution; 2) increasing numbers of Nicaraguans are fleeing both the violence of the bitter border wars and the increasingly inclusive government conscription; and 3) the *contras* themselves who have chosen to take up arms against the Sandinista government. While the latter two groups have become important only in the past few years, the plight of the indigenous groups is deeply rooted in the historic pattern of their relations with the Managua government. As several authors have observed, the conflict between the Sandinista government and the indigenous groups represents a collision between a revolutionary movement that interprets the world in class terms and envisions a powerful role for the state, on the one hand, and indigenous groups on the other hand who see the world in ethnic terms and insist on local autonomy.[42]

Nicaragua's indigenous groups are almost exclusively located in the province of Zelaya. While Zelaya occupies half of the country's territory, only 10 percent of the national population live there. Approximately 180,000 Mestizo peasants and a slightly smaller number of indigenous groups inhabit the region.[43]

At the time of the revolution, about 67,000 Miskitus, 700 Rama, 1,500 Gariphone or black Caribs, 5,000 Sumus, and 26,000 Afro-European descended Creoles lived in Zelaya. The Miskitus, as the largest of the ethnic groups, have traditionally lived in both Honduras and Nicaragua. During Nicaragua's colonial period, the British allied with the Miskitus to fight Spanish efforts to colonize the Mosquitia region. For more than two hundred years, a family line of kings, educated in Jamaica or England, presided over a coast loyal to the British Crown. The Miskitu used the British to build up their power vis à vis the other indigenous communities. By the mid-nineteenth century, Moravian missionaries had converted most of the Miskitus to Christianity. Through translations of hymns and the Bible and the establishment of strong religious communities, religion became a unifying element for the dispersed indigenous population.

However, with the independence of the Nicaraguan government, conflicts developed over the question of sovereignty. In 1860, Britain signed the Treaty of Managua with the Nicaraguan government, which created a Miskitu Reserve under Nicaraguan sovereignty with powers of local self-government granted to the Miskitu monarchy. Tellingly, this treaty was negotiated without the participation of any representative of the Miskitu crown. By 1880, the Miskitu king was granting concessions in timber and banana operations to North Americans and most of the region's trade was with the United States. Although there were some Miskitus who worked closely with César Agusto Sandino in fighting U.S. military occupation in the 1930s, many others identified with their employers and church leaders who saw him as a bandit. Over the years, the Nicaraguan government adopted very paternalistic attitudes toward the Miskitu population. While a certain level of autonomy was granted to the indigenous population, most Miskitus viewed their experiences with Spanish-speaking Nicaraguan governments in bitter terms.

For the most part, indigenous groups in both Nicaragua and Honduras have remained marginal to national politics, although the indigenous groups in Nicaragua have experienced more development. As Brown explains, "[t]here, the combination of a road link, more fertile land, and the bulk of the Indian population has led to the growth of small towns, a more or less active market system, and some commercial and social interaction with the interior. By contrast, Honduran Mosquitia seemed forgotten."[44]

During the revolutionary struggle, there were no clandestine organizations in Zelaya nor military encounters between revolutionary forces and Somoza's National Guard; thus no indigenous revolutionary leadership emerged to support the Sandinista government. When the FSLN came to power in 1979, the new leadership sought to incorporate the indigenous groups into the government. In 1979 the Nicaraguan government encouraged the formation of Misurasata, as the Nicaraguan Indian mass organization to represent the concerns of the Miskitu and other indigenous groups. Misurasata leaders saw this as an opportunity to call for concrete economic gains for the indigenous groups and to stress the innate superiority of Amerindian identity. In effect, Misurasata became an indigenous revitalization movement rather than an organization reflecting class consciousness. Even though the FSLN was largely drawn from the Pacific coast and lacked an understanding of the ethnic tensions on the Atlantic coast, during the first year of the revolutionary government relations were apparently quite good between the revolutionary government and the indigenous groups. In 1980, Misurasata presented the government with its list of demands, including the right to education in the indigenous language. Misurasata was subsequently given the right to be represented in the Nicaraguan Council of State as well as in other governmental agencies. Steadman Fagoth Mueller was selected by Misurasata to represent Indian national interests.

Problems began to develop between the Miskitus and the government at the conclusion of the Indians' literacy campaign, when the government interpreted Misurasata's "Plan 81" as a separatist movement with links to the CIA and the *contras* in Honduras. In February 1981, Fagoth and thirty other Misurasata activists were arrested by the Nicaraguan government; shortly thereafter, a number of Misurasata activists were killed in disputes with the government over the arrests of still more Misurasata leaders. In the wake of Fagoth's arrest, some 3,000 young Miskitu men crossed over into Honduras and joined the forces fighting the Sandinista regime. This produced still more antagonism between the government and the Indian community. The remaining members of the Misurasata Directorate, under the leadership of Brooklyn Rivera, presented a document to the government in July 1981, demanding political autonomy for the entire Department of Zelaya (almost half the country) to be run by Misurasata. The Sandinista government refused to negotiate such a demand, decertifying Misurasata as a legal organization and prompting still more Miskitus to join the *contras* in Honduras. Indeed, by late 1981, the *contras* had engaged in numerous terrorist acts against the Miskitu camps in an effort to rally them against the government.

The situation escalated to the point where in January and February 1982, the Nicaraguan government evacuated 16 Miskitu villages from the river border area, relocating the indigenous groups into five new settlements some 50 miles from the border (although well within the Miskitu traditional land area.) This forced relocation of 12,000 Miskitus created an international furor and condemnations of Nicaraguan brutality from both governments opposed to Nicaragua (the United States) and from groups hitherto supportive of the Nicaraguan revolution. In January 1982 U.S. Ambassador to the United Nations, Jeane Kirkpatrick, declared in a television interview that 250,000 Miskitus (four times their total population!) had been herded into concentration camps.[45]

In March 1982 several human rights groups visited the region but failed to find evidence of systematic human rights abuses.[46] At the time of the forced displacement of Miskitus into government-designated camps, more Nicaraguan Miskitus fled across the Honduran border to seek refuge, raising the total there to some 14,000.

By August 1982, most of Misurasata's leaders were in Honduras and Misurasata was renamed Misura and integrated into the *contra* FDN (National Democratic Forces). As the war became more brutal, Rivera broke with Fagoth and formed a rival *contra* organization which he called Misurasata and affiliated with ARDE (Revolutionary Democratic Alliance) in Costa Rica. As the violence increased in the border areas, more FSLN troops were sent to the indigenous regions where there were reports of serious human rights violations by government forces. And in fact, the Sandinista regime prosecuted and gave prison sentences to 44 soldiers for human rights violations against the indigenous population. Increasing awareness of the serious ethnic difficulties led to more sensitivity by the Sandinista forces, and by 1984, 70 percent of local security forces were from the Eastern coast while Pacific coast recruits were given training seminars before going to Zelaya.[47] But even as the FSLN forces were becoming more sensitive to the needs of the indigenous population, the *contra* forces were escalating the violence along the coastal areas.

For the Nicaraguan government, the issue of the Miskitus has been a difficult internal political question as well as an internationally embarrassing incident. As Bourgois points out, militarily the conflicts over ethnic minorities have produced very bitter fighting; politically, the accusations of human rights violations has damaged the regime's international image; and morally, the government's inability to incorporate minorities has contradicted the government's revolutionary principles.[48] Moreover, external forces—particularly the *contras*—have used legitimate grievances of the Miskitus as a lever against the Nicaraguan government.

Indeed, it is the politicization of the Miskitus' difficult relations with the Sandinista government that is further accentuating the problem. While the Sandinista government has announced an amnesty for members of indigenous groups currently living in Honduras to return, relatively few Miskitus have taken advantage of this offer. Given their past traditions of local autonomy and given their initial treatment at the hands of the Sandinistas, many Miskitus feel little loyalty to the FSLN regime. At the same time, the brutal war by the *contras*—supported by U.S. funds and advised by U.S. agents—has made the issue of the indigenous groups a question of national security for the Sandinista government. From their perspective, the Miskitus represent a serious security risk. The fact that so many Miskitus are fighting with the *contras* makes the issue more difficult. In October 1984, Brooklyn Rivera returned to Nicaragua to pursue peace talks with Daniel Ortega, now president of Nicaragua. Discussions over issues of indigenous land rights and local autonomy are continuing. However, Rivera's efforts to incorporate indigenous groups in Honduras into the negotiations have so far failed.

The violence of the *contras* has also displaced thousands of Nicaraguans within Nicaraguan territory. In 1985 the government initiated a program of return of the displaced to their communities. Together with the government's acceptance of a far-reaching program of regional autonomy for the Atlantic Coast region, these measures have substantially decreased tension within the country. But those groups returning to their home communities have found widespread destruction, and the Nicaraguan government lacks the economic resources to rebuild the affected communities. While many Nicaraguans, both indigenous groups and *ladinos*, have returned to their home communities, many more are willing to return but lack the economic resources to do so. Similarly, the continuing violence along the Honduran/Nicaraguan border has greatly complicated repatriation efforts of Miskitus from Honduras to Nicaragua.

The outrage expressed by U.S. officials over the mistreatment of Nicaraguan indigenous groups seems out of proportion to the damages inflicted. The accusations are also hypocritical in light of the government's silence about the massive counterinsurgency campaigns systematically conducted against indigenous groups in Guatemala. Not only have members of Nicaraguan indigenous groups sought safety from government persecution in Honduras, but growing numbers of ladino refugees are currently living along the Honduran/Nicaraguan border. The designation of these individuals as refugees is very controversial. Many of these individuals support the *contra* efforts to overthrow the Sandinista government. As discussed in the chapter on Honduras, the UNHCR has repeatedly limited the scope and nature of aid to these ladinos in an effort to prevent their manipulation by the *contra* forces. However, in February 1985, there were reports that the Reagan administration intended to supply aid to the *contra* forces—if Congress opposed covert aid—by increasing monetary assistance to the ladino refugees in Honduras. The politicization of both ladino and Miskitu refugees is thus very clear.

Furthermore, the flight of the Miskitus into Honduras has produced serious pressures on the Honduran government and has complicated an already complex refugee situation in that country. The Miskitus and the *contras* are the most widely publicized of the Nicaraguan groups leaving their country. But in both Costa Rica and Honduras, they have been joined by growing numbers of Nicaraguan civilians fleeing the brutality of the war with the *contras*. Large portions of both southern and northern Nicaragua have been terrorized by the *contras*. The Sandinista government has responded to the violence with more inclusive conscription, forced evacuation of civilians from the war zones into government-run camps, and intimidation of suspected *contra* supporters. These actions, together with the violence in the region and growing economic scarcity have produced a flood of Nicaraguans seeking security in the neighboring countries of Honduras and Costa Rica.

Before examining the responsibility of the host governments to the influx of Central American refugees, it is important to realize that the refugees are not a monolithic group. Not only do they come from different countries in response to different political/military situations but they come from different social groups. The final section of this chapter describes the Central American refugees themselves.

THE CENTRAL AMERICAN REFUGEES

As discussed above, those individuals who have left their countries are part of a much larger number of individuals displaced by the violence. In comparison with the internally displaced, the refugees crossing national boundaries tend to be more mobile and perhaps more educated than those remaining within their countries. The total number of refugees leaving their countries is very high; while estimates are extraordinarily difficult to obtain (given the fact that most refugees live in foreign countries without any legal permission to do so), Table 2.4 provides recent estimates for the number of Central American refugees in their countries of asylum.

Table 2.4: Central American Refugees, by Host Country

Country of Asylum	Total Number of Refugees	Major Groups	Numbers aided by UNHCR Jan. 1985
Mexico	200,000-250,000	Salvadorans 100,000-150,000; Guatemalans 100,000	43,000
Guatemala	50,000-100,000	Salvadorans 50,000-100,000	
Honduras	47,500	Salvadorans 30,000; Guatemalans 500; Nicaraguans 17,000	40,500
Nicaragua	22,000	Salvadorans 21,000; Guatemalans 500	1,770
Costa Rica	50,000	Salvadorans 23,500; Guatemalans 1,500; Nicaraguans 25,000	12,200
Belize	2,000	Salvadorans 2,000	2,000
Panama	1,500	Salvadorans 1,000	1,000
Dominican Republic			500
United States	585,000	Salvadorans 500,000; Guatemalans 35,000; Nicaraguans 50,000	

Source: UNHCR Fact Sheet, "Refugees in Central America and Belize," no. 12, January 1985; U.S. Senate Committee on the Judiciary, Subcommittee on Immigration and Refugee Policy, *Refugee Problems in Central America* (Washington, Government Printing Office, 1983); and personal interviews with governmental and nongovernmental officials in Washington, Mexico, Central America, and Geneva, 1984.

While it is difficult to secure reliable figures on the numbers of refugees, understanding the various types of refugees is essential to studying governmental refugee policies. Three principal groups of refugees may be identified:

a) The political exile: usually well-educated and from middle class backgrounds, this type of Central American fits the classic definition of refugee. Active in political organizations, trade unions, or other popular organizations, the political exile seeks asylum because he or she has been persecuted for political beliefs or activities. University professors, lawyers, intellectuals, and politicians—these individuals have been imprisoned, tortured, or threatened by the governments of their nations. For decades they have left Central America, seeking political asylum in Mexico, Costa Rica, the United States, and Europe. Their political persecution is clear and their educational and professional background has meant relatively fewer problems in adaptation to a new host country. R. L. Solomon studied the experiences of Guatemalan exiles and found that while most were frustrated by their inability to pursue political roles and by their difficulties in finding jobs commensurate with their educational backgrounds (three-fourths had college degrees), most ended up with jobs that provided for their economic security.[49] The number of political exiles leaving Central America seems to have remained fairly constant over the past decade with greater numbers leaving in the aftermath of military coups. Generally, these exiles have contacts in friendly countries and experience relatively little difficulty in comparison with other groups in obtaining political exile status or in supporting themselves.

b) The urban refugee: throughout the small towns and cities of El Salvador and Guatemala, thousands of individuals have chosen to leave their homes in search of increased security elsewhere. These people are generally of working class or lower middle class backgrounds, typically with jobs in the service sector or in small businesses. They usually decide to leave because they (or members of their families) have been politically visible—usually in an organization considered subversive by the present government (for example, an outlawed political party, a trade union, a peasant league). The level of seemingly random violence in the areas where they live may also inspire them to seek refuge elsewhere. Young men are the most likely urban population group to leave. Lacking the political clout of the upper classes to evade military service, young men in urban areas are likely to be pressed into military service—or even pressured from the left to join the guerrilla forces. Such pressures, coupled with the ever-present signs of violence—the corpses in the streets, the tales of torture and death from relatives and friends—lead many to leave their country. Reports from officials working in agencies providing services to refugees indicate a growing number of youth are leaving Nicaragua in order to evade military service. While Nicaragua has certainly not experienced the random violence of El Salvador and Guatemala, the militarization of the nation, coupled with rising casualty figures from border attacks, are apparently stimulating emigration.

Although they do not possess the resources of the "political exiles," the urban refugees may have contacts in urban areas of friendly countries and are able to make long journeys to obtain relative security. The journeys are typically arduous, expensive, and fraught with danger from both governmental security forces and from unscrupulous "coyotes" who guide them across the borders. Most in this group end up in Costa Rica, Mexico, or the United States. These "urban refugees" are distinguished from the "political exiles" in that they are usually not singled out for individual persecution based on their political activities. Word may get back to individuals that they are marked for death by a paramilitary death squad or by a group of soldiers—for no apparent reason. Having witnessed the fate of others similarly "marked," the individuals decide to avoid such danger and flee to other countries.

As residents of small towns, they seek urban areas in the host country and are unlikely to be enthusiastic about rural development projects set up by UNHCR or by agencies in the host country. Many of these refugees pass through Mexico on their way to the United States (and cause only minimal trouble to Mexico as their stay is temporary). Many will undoubtedly remain permanently in the host country—whether Costa Rica, Mexico, or the United States. Although their initial reasons for leaving their home countries were political, once they begin to create a new life in the recipient country—to get a job, to marry, to accumulate material possessions—they are less likely to return home. Certainly not all of the refugees will remain; indeed many count the days until return is possible. However, in comparison with the "political exiles" who almost invariably talk of returning when political conditions have changed, and the "peasants" who see returning home as their only option, the urban political migrant is much more likely to stay.

c) The peasant: peasants in both El Salvador and Guatemala have been the principal victims of the violence in their countries, perhaps because they are the largest group in both countries. Sometimes referred to as "crossfire refugees," they are driven from their homes by the violent actions of the government and rightwing paramilitary forces (and to a much lesser extent by leftist guerrilla forces). These people leave their homes reluctantly—usually only after having personally witnessed a massacre of civilians, death or disappearance of a family member, or the wanton destruction of their own or neighboring communities. Unlike the urban migrants, peasant refugees are predominantly women and children with a sprinkling of older people. Young men have generally already been killed, pressed into government service, joined the guerrillas, or otherwise fled the area. The peasants leave in groups; frequently whole communities set off in search of refuge. Their mobility is limited as they are usually illiterate (or in the case of Guatemalans may not speak Spanish), and generally have little knowledge of the world outside their borders. As one report noted, "Guatemalan peasants arriving in Mexico had never seen a television set nor could they name the capital city of their country."[50]

These peasants seek refuge in neighboring countries, generally as close to the borders as they feel safe or are allowed. They are at the mercy of the governments of the receiving country and may be forced to live in camps, to relocate, or even to return home. Peasant refugees are not only virtually powerless and inexperienced in dealing with governmental officials, but they lack that "mobility" that is characteristic of the other two groups. They wait in camps for a lessening of the violence and for the opportunity to return home. Their generally poor health conditions, coupled with the difficult circumstances under which they fled their homes, leaves them with serious health problems once they arrive in the country of refuge. Indeed, Walsh estimates that 10 percent of the Guatemalans arriving in Mexico die within the first few months of exile.[51] These health conditions and the refugees' almost total lack of resources create mammoth problems for already overburdened governments. Politically, they may antagonize local populations, producing a backlash against the refugees. Strategically, they complicate relations with neighboring states as the government of their country of origin always charges that they are guerrillas seeking a new location to continue the military struggle. When governments seek to move the refugees away from the border in response to these complications, the refugees resist relocation, preferring to remain closer to home so that if the violence subsides, their return will be easier.

The peasant refugees, then, cause the greatest immediate problem to the host governments while the urban migrants present a longer term set of difficulties. Political exiles create fewer problems—not only are they smaller in number, but their actions are more easily monitored by the governments. Their political activities may be circumscribed by the government and they may be deported if they become politically active in the host country.

Governments have responded to the presence of the Central American refugees in different ways. The following chapters explore the policies that governments have developed to respond to the influx of Central American refugees.

3

Mexico: The Politics of Ambiguity

Since 1980, the Mexican government has been faced with a growing influx of Central Americans fleeing the violence of their homelands.[1] Salvadorans travelling through Mexico on their way to the United States have frequently settled in Mexican cities while hundreds of thousands of Guatemalan peasants have crossed into the southern state of Chiapas, creating serious security problems with the Guatemalan armed forces. Proud of its long tradition of generous asylum policies and progressive foreign policies in the region, the Mexican government feels an obligation to accept and to care for the victims of the violence in El Salvador and Guatemala. At the same time, Mexico's economic difficulties and their political consequences mandate a much more restrictive immigration policy. These contradictory political and economic pressures together with the bureaucratic and personalist characteristics of Mexican policy-making, have resulted in confusing and ambiguous policies toward the estimated 250,000 Salvadorans and Guatemalans who have come to Mexico for political reasons.

The consequences of Mexican policies toward the refugees are very important in shaping the policies of other governments toward the refugees. The U.S. government, for example, has consistently denied Central American applications for political asylum on the grounds that these individuals could have stayed in Mexico, the country of first asylum. Thus, Mexico's policies toward the Central American refugees directly affect the number of Central Americans arriving in the United States and their treatment by the U.S. government. If Salvadorans were treated more generously by the Mexican government, it is possible that many would choose to remain in Mexico rather than travel on to the United States. Conversely, if Mexico's treatment of the refugees were more harsh, it might be more difficult for the U.S. government to deny refugee status on the grounds that the individual chose to leave his or her country of first asylum for economic reasons.

The Central American refugees are also a challenge to Mexican political stability. The issue of the government's treatment of refugees has become very politicized. Mexican conservatives fear the spread of revolution from Central America to Mexico and consequently want to limit the number of Central American migrants. The right is also fearful of the social, political, and economic impact of the large numbers of Central American migrants in Mexico and publicizes the threat they pose to Mexico in an effort to push the government toward more protectionist immigration policies. Thus PAN (Partido de Acción Nacional) spokesman Gerardo Medina warned that the "Central American fire could engulf us with this migration of undesirables."[2] Leopoldo Gonzalez Aguayo, General Coordinator of Research of the Facultad de Ciencias Políticas y Sociales of the Universidad Nacional Autónoma de México (UNAM) maintains that by the end of the decade, Mexico will have eight million foreigners within its borders and that the migration simply cannot be stopped.[3] Leftist critics of the regime point to inconsistencies in Mexican policies of opposing repressive regimes while being less than compassionate toward the victims of those regimes when they arrive in Mexico. Religious and humanitarian groups see in the refugees a means of making foreign policy issues more personal and more relevant to the general population. In fact, given the current economic crisis and growing political criticism of the government, the presence of the refugees could serve as a dangerous flashpoint.

Mexican policies toward the refugees are a function of many factors. In the sections that follow, Mexico's political culture, foreign policy objectives, economic situation, and the nature of the refugee flows are examined. In tracing these connections, the reasons for the ambiguity in Mexican policies become clear.

THE REVOLUTIONARY HERITAGE

Mexico's political culture is dominated by its revolutionary tradition. The 1910 revolution destroyed the power of the landed oligarchy and the church and reduced the power of the industrialists and foreign interests. During the turbulent period following the seven-year insurrection, a new political order was established that reflected the power of the various revolutionary forces. The Mexican political system that emerged from the revolutionary epoch has been a surprisingly stable one. The establishment of a single party, the Partido Revolucionario Institutionalizado (PRI) served to incorporate the principal revolutionary groups (particularly the peasants and the unions) into a governing coalition. This process of cooptation—at which Mexican political leaders have become amazingly adept—has served as an effective means of social control. Although the government has never hesitated to use force against dissidents it could not coopt (as in the 1968 massacre at Tlatelolco), the government has relied primarily on cooptation to maintain stability.

The Mexican government[4] is dominated by the president, who has extensive formal powers and even more extensive informal powers through his control of patronage. The development of strong, stable political institutions in both the party and the presidency has enabled successive Mexican governments to ease the military out of politics. Unlike virtually all other Latin American nations, the Mexican military has, by and large, remained on the political sidelines. This has been possible due to clever manipulation by civilian elites, to the increasing legitimacy of civilian political institutions, and to the regime's successful use of ideology. The ideology of the revolution has been skillfully and pervasively used by all Mexican governments to build popular support for their policies. All governments and all political leaders—right and left—proudly proclaim their allegiance to the revolution. The myth of the revolution is a powerful component of the government's ruling coalition. It has served to justify and legitimize many actions that would otherwise be interpreted as conservative or even reactionary.

As many observers have noted, in recent years the Mexican government has become increasingly conservative in its domestic policies. In spite of the rhetoric of the revolution, inequality has become more blatant, the political system has become increasingly corrupt, and society has become more resistant to change. The present political system seems out of touch with the revolutionary ideals that inspired it. But the ideology and the myth of the revolution live on and are used to justify and legitimize increasingly conservative governmental actions. The Mexican government has traditionally used support for revolutionary governments abroad as a means of compensating for its fundamentally conservative policies at home. And there is real and substantial popular support for revolutionary movements abroad among most segments of public opinion. This revolutionary heritage has not only shaped Mexican national political institutions and foreign policy, but has also had a direct impact on Mexico's attitudes toward political dissidents.

Mexico has a long tradition of providing political asylum to individuals persecuted for their political beliefs. Leon Trotsky sought asylum from Mexico as did thousands of Spaniards fleeing Franco's authoritarian regime. Later waves of political leaders opposing dictatorial Latin American governments sought refuge in Mexico. Mexico is justly proud of its heritage as a haven for political dissidents. But this refuge was largely extended to professionals and intellectuals who had been political leaders in their own countries. In the late 1970s a different type of political refugee began to arrive as the direct result of the changing nature of political violence in Central America as well as improved international communications and transportation. While coups d'etat had previously resulted in the expulsion of a relatively small number of political leaders, beginning in 1980 thousands of Salvadorans came to Mexico seeking sanctuary from the violence of their country's revolution. They were followed by hundreds and thousands, and then hundreds of thousands, of Guatemalan peasants fleeing the brutal counterinsurgency campaigns of their government. While Mexico had traditionally given asylum to many of Central America's politically active professionals throughout this century, the current waves of refugees pose very different problems. The Guatemalans were peasants, usually illiterate, and from rural indigenous communities. The Salvadorans (and some Guatemalans) were from working class backgrounds and from the small towns in those countries. Mexican policymakers were unprepared for the influx of refugees, and the policies they developed toward the refugees reflect that lack of preparation.

Mexican political leaders since World War II have defined Mexico's role in the world in terms of support for international law and organization; that commitment to a just world order based on law is part of Mexico's political culture. And yet, Mexico is not a signatory to the UN Conventions on refugees and does not recognize a refugee status within its immigration law. Indeed, the Mexican government argues that Mexican domestic legislation offers sufficient protection for refugees and that there is no need to ratify additional international agreements on the subject.[5] Several government officials privately express fears that Mexican ratification of the UN agreements would obligate the government to accept undesirable groups such as Somocistas from Nicaragua or exiles from Cuba or even Indochinese refugees. Such a restriction on Mexican freedom is politically unacceptable. It does not seem likely that Mexico will ratify the UN conventions in the near future. As one Mexican official stated, "it would have been easier to do so five years ago. Now with a quarter of a million Central American refugees already here and more wanting to come, it is just about impossible."[6] In this case, Mexico's tradition of support for international law has been tempered by other concerns. Mexico's foreign policy objectives have also had an impact on Mexico's domestic political culture, tradition, and its commitments to principles of international law.

AN INDEPENDENT FOREIGN POLICY TRADITION

Mexican foreign policy has been shaped by the country's geographic location bordering the United States and, since 1910, by the revolutionary imperative. Mexico's struggle to define its relationship with the United States since independence has been extensively studied.[7] When Mexico achieved its independence from Spain in 1821, its power was not significantly different from that of the United States. The two nations were approximately equal in population and land size. However, that balance changed very rapidly. The movement for Texan independence, followed quickly by the Mexican-American War established U.S. dominance over Mexico. The Treaty of Guadalupe Hidalgo in 1848 formally gave the United States about half of Mexico's territory, including parts of present-day California, Arizona, Colorado, Nevada, New Mexico, and Utah. This memory of Mexico's defeat and humiliation at the hands of the "Colossus of the North" has been an important determinant of Mexico's political culture. Throughout the nineteenth century, the United States intervened in Mexican politics with relative impunity. During the Mexican revolution, U.S. president Woodrow Wilson intervened both militarily and politically in the revolutionary process, supporting some factions over others and trying to determine the revolution's outcome. Border attacks by Pancho Villa on the United States followed by border attacks by General Pershing on Mexico. In fact, relations between the two governments sank to new lows during the revolutionary period.

Relations between the United States and Mexico's revolutionary government were tense and complicated over the issue of Mexican compensation for expropriated property belonging to U.S. citizens and later by the strongly negative U.S. reaction of Mexican president Lazaro Cardenas' nationalization of the Mexican oil industry. Although the United States applied strong diplomatic pressure in response to the nationalization, the U.S. response was mitigated by the fact that in 1938, U.S. attention was directed toward Europe. The United States and Mexico cooperated quite closely during the war; the initiation of the *bracero* program to regularize the temporary migration of Mexican workers into the United States was begun at this time. Since World War II, Mexican relations with the United States have been characterized by periods of tension over border-related issues and migration and by Mexico's continued economic dependence on the United States. Currently, Mexico depends on the United States for approximately two thirds of its international economic transactions (trade, investment, tourism, and so on). As will be discussed below, Mexico's current economic crisis and monumental foreign debt have further tied Mexico to the United States. Given Mexico's proximity to, and its economic and cultural dependence on the United States, the importance that Mexico attaches to relations with the U.S. becomes understandable. Many Mexican authors have analyzed the extent to which Mexico's national character has been shaped by its northern neighbor.[8] Through experience, Mexico has become extremely sensitive to U.S. efforts to intervene in Mexican politics. U.S. statements and actions are analyzed in careful detail for signs of pressure or intimidation.

Mexican struggles to define itself vis à vis the United States have been particularly evident in its foreign policy. Combining its revolutionary traditions with its need to demonstrate independence from the United States, Mexico has developed an activist foreign policy supportive of Third World aspirations and of revolutionary movements in particular. Mexican commitment to nonintervention—itself the product of historical experiences with an interventionist power—has shaped the nature of Mexican foreign policy. For example, Mexico announced the Estrada doctrine in 1930 in which Mexico grants diplomatic recognition to any government regardless of its ideological orientation or means of achieving power. This was a clear reaction to U.S. efforts to use diplomatic recognition as a tool for influencing the outcomes of the Mexican revolution. Mexico strongly and vociferously opposed U.S. intervention in Guatemala in 1954, in the Dominican Republic in 1965, and in Chile in 1970. Mexico's historic support for nonintervention and its efforts to assert its independence from the United States have led it to adopt very supportive policies vis à vis international organizations and international law. Like other small powers, Mexico has sought to limit the exercise of power by more powerful states through support for international norms limiting force. Similarly, Mexico has sought to balance its overwhelming dependence on the United States with a diversification of its foreign relations. Mexico has eagerly increased its ties with other nations to counterbalance the United States. Relations with Europe have been expanded and ties with the socialist bloc have been emphasized.

Mexico's relations with Cuba are perhaps the clearest manifestation of Mexico's search for independence vis à vis the United States. In spite of U.S. pressure, Mexico was the only Latin American nation to maintain diplomatic and trade relations with Cuba from 1964 to 1970. Mexico has taken many opportunities to urge the re-incorporation of Cuba into the inter-American community and to support Cuba's revolutionary ideology. As many scholars have noted, Mexican support for Cuba's revolutionary government has served a very important domestic function as well. Support for revolution abroad has been a relatively low-cost way for Mexico to emphasize its revolutionary heritage—especially in light of its increasingly conservative domestic policies—and to coopt leftist opposition to the regime. By adhering to a pro-Cuba policy, the Mexican government has ensured that its leftist opponents could not use this issue to criticize the government.

Mexican foreign policy has thus been a curious blend of support for progressive movements abroad with the need to maintain good relations with the United States. At times, these opposing foreign policy objectives have resulted in contradictory foreign policies. These contradictions have been especially acute in the case of Central America.[9] In discussing Mexico-Central American relations, most observers assume that Central America is Mexico's natural sphere of influence and that Mexico has a long tradition of influence in the region. Yet the historical record is much more ambiguous. In spite of several efforts by Mexican politicians to intervene in Guatemalan politics, and the much-heralded Mexican support for Nicaraguan revolutionary César Agosto Sandino in the 1930s, the fact is that Mexico has historically paid very little attention to Central America. No Mexican president, for example, ever visited a Central American country until 1966.

Commercial relations between Mexico and Central America have historically been of only minor importance. During World War II when U.S.-Mexican trade was disrupted, Mexico increased its trade with Central America, reaching a high of 16 percent of its total trade. However by 1950 U.S. dominance had been resurrected and Mexico's trade with Central America declined. In the mid 1960s, Mexican President Díaz Ordaz sought to increase exports to Central America and to foster greater cooperation with the nations of the region. And under President Luis Echeverría (1970-1976), Mexico and Central American nations signed many economic agreements. And yet, economically, Mexico had very little stake in Central America; its interests were overwhelmingly with the United States. On a political level, there were obvious difficulties with Mexico aligning too closely with the rightwing military governments that dominated the region. Mexico, trying to assert its progressive international image, did not want to be perceived as accepting what it viewed as repressive governments.

Relations with Guatemala have always been difficult. For Guatemala, Mexico is the "Colossus of the North." As discussed in the preceding chapter, border disputes have troubled relations between the two countries since independence in the 1820s. As a bordering nation, Guatemala poses a special set of difficulties for the Mexican government. Mexico is much more reluctant to intervene in Guatemalan affairs and is much more cautious about upsetting Guatemalan leaders than leaders of the other Central American nations.

In Central America, Mexico has tried to shore up its revolutionary credentials and, in a sense, to repeat its experience with Cuba. Olga Pellicer, one of the foremost scholars on Mexican foreign policy, maintains that Mexico is expected to "act as a force to inhibit [North] American interventionist tendencies, [to] . . . support revolutionary governments, and [to] . . . promote the establishment in the region of Central America and the Caribbean basin, of an international order that would permit the coexistence of regimes with a plurality of ideological, economic, and political orientations."[10]

Mexico clearly fears U.S. military intervention in Central America and seeks to prevent this from happening. U.S. intervention in Central America would raise the possibility of U.S. intervention elsewhere. While rejecting the domino theory, Mexican foreign-policy leaders are concerned about the destabilizing effects of the Central American revolutions on the Mexican polity. Mexico sees structural change in Central America as a force for long-term stability in the region. By supporting such change, Mexico sees itself as not only deflecting attention away from Mexico's growing domestic problems, but also as containing the spread of violence in Central America.

With the Nicaraguan revolution, the Mexican government was under considerable pressure to support the revolution. In 1979, Mexico abandoned the Estrada Doctrine in breaking relations with Somoza's regime. Since the Sandinista victory, Mexico has been one of the regime's greatest supporters. Politically, Mexico has supported the revolution and has tried to use its influence with the United States to moderate conflicts there. Mexican presidents López Portillo and Miguel de la Madrid have both clearly and unambiguously tied Mexico to the Sandinista government. Economically, Mexico has extended substantial financial support to the Sandinistas. As Pellicer notes, between 1979 and 1981 Mexico extended $72,900,000 in bilateral loans to Nicaragua—a figure totaling 14 percent of the total loans received by Nicaragua and exceeded only by those from Libya. Moreover, during the same period Mexico made outright grants of $39,509,900 or 21 percent of total aid received.[11] Through the Acuerdo de San José, Mexico joined with Venezuela in selling oil at what were essentially subsidized rates to Central American countries, including Nicaragua.

Although Mexico has not broken relations with the Salvadoran government, Mexican support for the Salvadoran revolutionary movements there is clear. The headquarters of the FMLN/FDR (Frente Farabundo Martí de Liberación Nacional/Frente Democrático Revolucionario) are in Mexico City, and the Mexican government has provided both political asylum and financial support for the revolutionaries. In August 1981, Mexico joined with French president François Mitterrand in urging a political solution to El Salvador's violence and calling for the inclusion of the FDR in the negotiating process. Mexico suffered considerable diplomatic criticism; not only did the United States and El Salvador reject this move, but most Latin American governments saw such a suggestion as inherently interventionist. And there have been contradictions in Mexico's policies toward the revolutionary movements; while Mexico is extending moral and political support to the revolutionaries, Mexico's sales of subsidized oil to the Salvadoran government in 1980 amounted to a $73,000 per day subsidy to the Salvadoran government.[12]

Moreover, Mexican support for the Salvadoran revolutionaries was never paralleled by support for the Guatemalan revolutionary forces. When pressed on this point, Mexican officials explain that this is because the Guatemalan forces are much further from victory than their Salvadoran counterparts. And yet, the formation of a unified Guatemalan opposition force would make such a policy at least possible.

During the past two years, most of Mexico's energies in Central America have been directed at the Contadora Group in which Mexico, Venezuela, Colombia, and Panama have pressured for a political solution to the region's conflicts. They have sought to force all parties involved in the conflict to negotiate their differences—both internally and between nations (for example, Costa Rica and Nicaragua). The Contadora process has been plagued with problems, most notably the opposition of the United States, the unwillingness of several of the belligerent parties to accept the intervention of outside forces, and perhaps most fundamentally the inability of the Contadora process even to understand the situation in common terms. Thus while the Salvadoran and Guatemalan governments persistently portray their opposition as externally funded and directed, the revolutionary groups see themselves as representing the legitimate aspirations of their people. Under the de la Madrid administration (1982–), Mexico appears to be attempting to share some of the risk in adopting progressive policies toward the region. Given Mexico's profound economic problems, which have triggered a greater awareness of Mexico's political and economic vulnerability to the United States, it is perhaps reasonable to expect Mexico to be more cautious through adoption of a multilateral regional approach. Mexico's policies toward Central America are undoubtedly tempered by its need to maintain good relations with the United States. U.S. officials have publicly and privately sought to persuade Mexico to support Washington's initiatives in Central America, and there is evidence that Mexican policies toward Central America are, in fact, becoming more moderate.[13]

There are indications that Mexico's support for the Nicaraguan revolution is tapering off. Mexico has reduced shipments of oil to Nicaragua to minimal amounts and has at times suspended them for several months.[14] Furthermore, following revelation of CIA mining of Nicaragua's harbors in 1984, the Mexican government refused the French request in private conversations to support French and other European moves to sweep Nicaragua's port.

Relations with Guatemala have been particularly difficult. Aguilar argues that "[i]n its attempts to intimidate Mexico, Guatemala's biggest ally is the United States"[15] and that both countries are using all available means to dissuade Mexico from its policy of support from the Mexican revolutionaries. While the Guatemalan government insists that its concern is due to the fact that arms are being smuggled into Guatemala via the Mexican border, relations have always been tense because of the long shared border. In March 1982 Benedicto Lucas García, then Guatemalan army chief of staff and brother of the president, asked the Mexican government to collaborate in guaranteeing border security. In a not-too-veiled insult, Lucas García remarked that "Perhaps the Mexican authorities are not sufficiently strong to stop subversive activities on the border, which is why I consider a greater militarization of the Mexican side of the border to be advisable."[16] For Mexico, the security threats have come from the Guatemalan military forces, not from the increasing migration of Guatemalans. Significantly, the Mexican government has never seen the Guatemalan refugees inside its territory as guerrillas fighting against the Guatemalan regime. Relations between the two countries have been tense due to political difficulties between the two regimes, the presence of large numbers of Guatemalan refugees in Mexico, and the difficulties of patrolling the borders. Moreover, there have been cases where Mexican officials have "disappeared" in Guatemala and increasingly frequent border violations by the Guatemalan government. These border incidents are discussed below in the context of the political consequences of the refugee migrations.

As the economic and political situation in Mexico deteriorates, it becomes more important than ever for the Mexican government to stress its revolutionary commitment. As discussed in the section below, the political consequences of the economic crisis are serious and serve to limit Mexico's ability to respond to the refugees.

ECONOMIC CRISIS

Since 1982, Mexico has suffered serious economic problems that have limited its policy options toward the refugees. Mexico's well-publicized economic crisis stems in part from the distortions resulting from exploitation of its vast oil reserves. Since the oil has been exploited, governmental revenues have increased, governmental spending and investment have skyrocketed, and Mexico has become more dependent on oil exports. In 1977, oil made up 22 percent of all Mexican exports; by 1981, it accounted for 75 percent.[17] But development of the oil required huge capital investments in technology, which in turn led to increasing foreign debt. Indeed by 1982, Mexico had become the world's largest debtor, owing an estimated $85 billion to foreign bankers. The dislocations caused by the 1981 oil glut brought into sharp relief the structural deficiencies of the Mexican system. The government was forced to renegotiate its debt payment schedule, necessitating the adoption of austerity measures, including raising taxes, cutting wages and services, decreasing subsidies on basic necessities, and sharply curtailing public expenditures. Inflation has been high, unemployment has increased, and businesses have suffered their highest bankruptcy rates. The Mexican economy remains in serious trouble and the government of Miguel de la Madrid has had to concentrate its energies on resolving the financial crisis and restoring national economic security. The expectations created by the increased oil revenues coupled with revelations of massive governmental corruption during the López Portillo administration created profound public cynicism and dissatisfaction with the government. While by early 1984 the de la Madrid administration had received high marks within the international financial community for its compliance with the austerity programs, the political costs of such compliance have been high. Because Mexico has implemented the required austerity programs, the U.S. government and the IMF have supported the Mexican government in easing the timetables for debt repayment. But the political costs of being a "model debtor" have been high. In 1983, the economy experienced an inflation rate of 78 percent and a drop of 8.5 percent in its GDP.[18] The *Wall Street Journal* reported in May 1984 that in spite of its much heralded economic programs, the Mexican government has still not recovered the 30 percent real drop in the standard of living of the population.[19] The political consequences of the economic crisis have been serious. PRI is losing popularity among the middle and upper classes because of its austerity program, and the principal conservative opposition party, PAN, appears to be picking up strength.[20]

The September 20, 1985 earthquake in Mexico increased economic hardship. The monumental financial cost of rebuilding the damaged parts of the city made it unlikely that Mexico would be able to meet its scheduled debt repayments.

On a more general level, the economic crisis has made it even more imperative that revolutionary elements be coopted and that opposition be controlled by the government. There is considerable speculation in

Mexico that the United States is taking advantage of Mexico's weak economic position to pressure Mexico into adopting a foreign policy more compatible with U.S. interests in the region. Furthermore, the tremendous domestic economic pressures limit the government's financial resources. With respect to the Central American refugees, the economic situation mandates a restrictive policy toward immigration while Mexico's foreign policy traditions put pressure on the government to be generous toward the refugees.

Although its policies are inconsistent in several respects, Mexico prides itself on its progressive, even revolutionary, foreign policies in the region. But those progressive foreign policies have been sorely tested by the Central American refugees. It is one thing to support revolutionary movements in Central America; it is quite another to provide for a quarter of a million unskilled laborers seeking security, food, and jobs in Mexico—particularly when Mexico is in the midst of its severest financial crisis to date. Miguel de la Madrid's support for a negotiated settlement through the efforts of the Contadora group is based on the realization that a political solution is essential for resolving regional conflicts and the refugees they produce.

THE REFUGEES IN MEXICO

There are three distinct groups of Central American refugees in Mexico, each posing a different set of problems for the government.

(1) Salvadorans and Guatemalans in transit to the United States: At least 50,000 Central Americans are using Mexico as a "trampoline" to the United States. Although least problematical to the Mexican government because they make the fewest demands for services, these refugees raise the thorny issue of cooperation between Mexican and U.S. immigration officials in deporting the refugees back to Central America. In fact, Mexican vigilance in the north is stronger than in the south. However, the Mexican government prefers that such cooperation be kept at a low profile. Recent reports indicate that passage through Mexico is becoming more costly and more difficult for Central American refugees. Many so-called "coyotes" have exploited the desperation of the refugees, and the human costs of getting to the U.S. side of the border are growing.

(2) Salvadorans and Guatemalans living primarily in Mexican cities: There are an estimated 100,000 Central American refugees living throughout Mexico—most without any official recognition. Only a handful (perhaps 500) of the Central Americans have been granted political asylum. Brill reports that in 1982, Mexico granted legal status to 72 individuals referred to it by the UNHCR; in 1983, to 151.[21] This has put the Mexican government in conflict with the UNHCR, which

wishes to see more Central Americans granted political exile status. In fact, UNHCR representative Pierre Jambor was declared persona non grata by the Mexican government in 1983 because of his zealous advocacy of the refugees' cause.

The lack of legal status means that most of the refugees come to Mexico on six-month tourist cards that were, until recently, easily obtained from airlines and travel agencies outside Mexico.[22] Others live with false documentation or enter the murky world of workers "without papers" in Mexico. Although prohibited from living in Mexico City (due to the already overwhelming pressures of the city's 17 million inhabitants), an estimated 40,000 Salvadorans are presently living in the capital city. Most of these refugees come from Salvadoran and Guatemalan cities and small towns; many are young men who have come to Mexico out of fear of being pressed into military duty on the one hand or into the guerrilla forces on the other. Officials in Mexican relief organizations report that many in this group will probably settle in Mexico. While Central Americans in this group place many demands on the system (employment, education, health services, and so forth), the Mexican government provides no direct services to the refugees. The few refugee relief centers in urban areas are sponsored by nongovernmental organizations. Refugee political organizations and solidarity committees are very active in Mexico City for both Salvadorans and Guatemalans.

(3) Guatemalan peasants seeking to settle along the border: The approximately 100,000 Guatemalan peasants who came to Mexico's southern provinces (principally Chiapas) are very different from the refugees who have travelled to the cities. Overwhelmingly rural and from indigenous groups (95 percent speak indigenous languages), these peasants arrive with their families and occasionally their entire communities to seek temporary protection from the violence back home. They generally arrive destitute, malnourished, and frequently wounded or sick as well. Officially, 40,000 refugees are registered and until 1984, lived within the forty camps and two "officially designated" zones. But most observers estimate an additional 60,000 Guatemalan refugees live in the area in addition to those in the camps.[23] This is the most problematical of the three groups for the Mexican government. The refugees depend almost completely on the Mexican government (and the nongovernmental organizations that work through the government) for food, housing, and services. Conditions in the camps have also exposed the government to criticism from both domestic and foreign sources. Moreover, the refugees have proved to be a constant source of tension for Mexico's already troubled relations with Guatemala. There have been numerous military incidents along the border in which Mexicans as well as refugees have been killed by Guatemalan security forces in pursuit of presumed

guerrillas crossing the border into Mexico. While the refugees generally see their stay in Mexico as temporary, and thus do not appear to pose the threat of permanently increasing Mexico's population, the political difficulties they cause put serious pressures on the government.

The political and economic pressures on the government are particularly acute in the state of Chiapas, the Mexican state that borders Guatemala and which until recently housed most of the Guatemalan refugees. Living conditions in Chiapas are worse than in the nation as a whole. Illiteracy rates in Chiapas are 29 percent (compared with the national average of 15 percent), only 36 percent of the homes have electricity (national average is 73 percent), and 45 percent have piped water (national average is 71 percent).[24] Some Mexican officials worry that the increased economic hardships posed by both the national economic crisis and by the presence of the refugees will provide a hospitable environment for the revolutionary ideas presumably brought by the refugees. The fear of revolution coupled with the substantial economic costs on the state of Chiapas have created a tense situation that the government would like to contain.

In developing its policies toward the refugees, Mexico has had to take into consideration the different needs and the different political repercussions of each of the three groups of Central American refugees.

MEXICO'S POLICIES TOWARD THE REFUGEES

Mexico's ambiguous policy toward the Central American refugees reflects these contradictory pressures. In general, the government refuses to recognize the Central Americans as refugees and to give them the guarantees—particularly legalization of their presence and assurances that they will not be returned—that such a recognition of status implies.

At the same time the Mexican government is under considerable pressure to formulate policies toward the Central Americans streaming across its borders that are consistent with Mexican traditions of political asylum and with its progressive foreign policy image. Consequently, Mexico tacitly accepts the Central American refugees and generally allows them to live within its territory. Along its southern border, the Mexican government has established camps for the refugees administered through a governmental agency, COMAR (Comisión Mexicana de Ayuda a Refugiados). COMAR was established in 1981 to coordinate Mexican policies toward the refugees, to administer the camps, and generally to serve as an advocate for the refugees within the Mexican bureaucracy. Nongovernmental organizations such as Oxfam, Catholic Relief Services, the Mexican Friends Service Committee, and various European organizations, as well as the UNHCR, have been active in providing funds. The government, however, has maintained control over the camps, and the activities of nongovernmental organizations have been much more limited than in other Central American nations.

Mexico has discouraged further refugee migration by providing only minimal services in the camps, and virtually no services in urban areas, for the refugees. Hunger, disease, and infant mortality rates are high within the camps, even by comparison with already high rates normal of Guatemalan and Mexican rural areas. Provision of needed services is particularly inadequate in the small outlying camps.[25] Mexican officials point out, though, that there is much poverty and hunger among Mexicans also, particularly in Chiapas, the southern state where most of the camps are located. Providing adequately for the refugees could trigger further resentment on the part of local populations who are not well-served themselves. A study by the U.S. General Accounting Office reports that in the past three years, Mexican government funding of refugee assistance programs has decreased from $1,800,000 in 1982 to $180,000 in 1983 and to an estimated $55,000 in 1984. In fact, the GAO concludes that the lack of adequate assistance to the refugees in Mexico encourages their migration to the United States.[26]

In addition the Central American refugees have virtually no legal protection. Except for the handful of Central Americans who are given political asylum, the refugees live in constant insecurity. The Mexican government deports between 600 and 1,000 Central American illegal immigrants weekly; there is no way of determining who are "refugees" and who are "economic migrants."[27] There are also occasional mass deportations of Guatemalans from camps. The largest deportations occurred May 20 and July 19, 1981, when approximately 3,000 Guatemalans were forced to leave Mexico.[28] In February 1982, 630 Guatemalans were deported, while the president of COMAR was saying: "I refuse to believe that this has happened. This Commission was especially created by the president to deal with such situations."[29] However, these situations appear to derive more from spontaneous decisions made by particular officials within the bureaucracy than from official policy.[30] As the vast majority of Central Americans living in Mexico are doing so without legal recognition by the government, the deportations cause widespread fear and uncertainty.

Along the border until 1984 registered refugees were given immigration documents permitting them to go back and forth across the border for 90 days; however this document, the so-called FM-8, gives permission neither to work in Mexico nor to travel beyond the 150-kilometer border zone. As mentioned above, many refugees living within the cities have used tourist cards to enter the country, renewing them every six months from outside the country. However in the spring of 1983 the

Mexican government imposed new restrictions on the use of tourist cards for residents of Central American and certain Caribbean nations. Residents of these countries can now be issued tourist cards only from the Mexican consulates in their countries of residence. Under the new regulations, therefore, Central Americans must now return to their own countries in order to secure legal authorization to re-visit Mexico. Clearly this is impossible for most Central American refugees. To return to their home countries means exposing themselves to the violent situation they fled from in the first place.[31] By making refugee status—or even de facto status—unattractive, the Mexican government is seeking to reduce the flow of refugees. Leaders of the refugee political groups also fear that the government is trying to intimidate such groups from becoming more politically active, and from criticizing Mexican policy.

On April 30, 1984, Guatemalan military forces attacked El Chupadero refugee camp in Chiapas, killing six refugees and destroying several villages. The following day, May 1, Secretary of the Interior Manuel Bartlett announced that the refugees would be moved for their own protection to camps further from the border. This decision, it was announced, was in accord with the standard practices of the UNHCR, which always prefers to guarantee the security of refugees by moving them away from the border. As the land situation in Chiapas was so difficult, with no free land available for settlement by refugees, the government purchased land farther away in Campeche and Quintana Roo for refugee camps. The Mexican government has made it very clear that its decision in this matter is final and that it would not tolerate any discussion of the decision. The UNHCR was not included in the decision-making process itself although it had been involved in earlier discussions of alternative campsites for the refugees.

The issue immediately became politicized as many refugees indicated that they were unwilling to move. The refugees were unsure about what kind of camp they were going to and wished to remain close to the border to facilitate their eventual return home. Many refugees—including the 2,500 at the Puerto Rico camp—simply refused to move. The Mexican government was not at all sympathetic to the resistance on the part of the refugees. On July 2 the Mexican government announced that only members of the armed forces or COMAR could enter the jungle. On July 3 the Puerto Rico camp was burned, including all the housing and food warehouses; moreover Mexican government officials said that no more food would be given to the refugees unless they moved. Mexican navy personnel—who were responsible for transporting the refugees—burned canoes used by the refugees so that they could not go out looking for food. Efforts to intimidate the refugees made the situation very uncomfortable. Nongovernmental organizations urged the government to be more responsive to the refugees' concerns, but tension between the groups increased. Approximately 2,000 Guatemalan refugees left El Chupadero for La Gloria—a spontaneous refugee settlement in the jungle—to avoid moving to Campeche.

Although the move was extremely controversial and physically difficult at the beginning, due to the short notice for implementing the transfer (which was accelerated because of the Guatemalan military attack), within several months the situation had been stabilized. By January 1985 approximately half of the refugees had been transferred from the Chiapas camps to the new camps in Campeche and Quintana Roo. (The estimated 60,000 Guatemalans living in the jungle outside the camps, however, remained in Chiapas.) Once the refugees in Chiapas learned that conditions there were quite comfortable and much more secure than in Chiapas, the other refugees moved with much less resistance. The relocation eased the immediate security problem along the border and did much to de-politicize a situation that had become virtually impossible.

Although the Mexican government still publicly affirms its intention to move the remaining refugees from their Chiapas camps to the new sites, it seems unlikely that they will all, in fact, be moved. Given the economic costs of doing so and the low number of new Guatemalan entrants, the government seems tacitly to accept the present situation.

Considerable speculation remains, however, that the Mexican government may negotiate some form of a repatriation scheme with the Guatemalan government. The meeting between de la Madrid and then President Mejía Victores in late 1985 led to fears that a more permanent solution for the refugees—in the form of repatriation—might be in the offing.

The relocation experience illustrates the dominant position of the government in the refugee policymaking process; the UNHCR and nongovernmental organizations were completely excluded from the process. In spite of the publicity surrounding the relocation, the Mexican government has continually sought to downplay the whole issue of the refugees. The refugees are politically controversial, and the government seeks to avoid further controversy by limiting public access to the camps. The presence of the military has reportedly increased in the region, along with tighter control over refugee movements.[32] The de la Madrid administration appears to be tightening its refugee policies, while at the same time it seeks to diminish public awareness of the refugee situation.

POLITICAL INFLUENCES ON THE REFUGEE POLICYMAKING PROCESS

Within the Mexican government there have been strong, contradictory pressures regarding treatment of Central American refugees. The traditional foreign policy concerns of nonintervention, support of revolutionary movements, and desire for consistency in foreign policy are represented by the Ministry of Foreign Relations (Secretaría de Relaciones Exteriores). The domestic economic crisis, together with the pressure to keep down migration of all kinds, including that of refugees, is the concern of the Ministry of the Interior (Secretaría de Gobernacion). Traditionally, national security concerns and the responsibility to maintain a secure border are the province of the military and the Ministry of Defense. There is also the coordinating agency mentioned before, the Mexican Commission for Refugee Aid (Comisión Mexicana de Ayuda a Refugiados, or COMAR), whose function is to coordinate overall Mexican policy and at the same time to provide both aid and political representation for the refugees. Finally, there are intense political pressures experienced by all the ministries and organizations concerned.

Conflicting pressures have produced inconsistent policies. Depending on who has had the upper hand at any particular moment, refugees have been either deported, given direct aid through refugee camps, been given political exile status (occasionally), or ignored as they entered the ambiguous world of the illegal immigrant in Mexico. Overriding all the inconsistencies, however, has been the strong desire of the government to divert attention from the situation, to adopt low-profile policies which, at one and the same time, both discourage further immigration while trying to provide a measure of relief to those already within the country. Both the López Portillo administration (1976–1981) and the current de la Madrid administration (1982–) have maintained that the refugee problem is primarily a political problem, whose solution will depend upon finding a solution to the violence afflicting Central America. Thus, policymaking in Mexico is shaped by the different bureaucratic interests of the involved agencies and ministries, by the underlying political pressures, and by the personalist nature of Mexican government, which affects the policymaking process itself.

The Foreign Ministry wants refugee policies to be consistent with the nation's foreign policies of support for progressive forces in Central America. And yet the Mexican government is clearly not ready to break diplomatic relations with Guatemala, nor to recognize the revolutionary groups there as a provisional government. Guatemalan guerrilla forces are perceived to be far from achieving a military victory. The Foreign Ministry thus supported the decision to move the refugees away from the

Guatemalan border as a way of defusing tension with the Guatemalan government. Mexico's policies toward the Central American refugees are also affected by its relations with the United States. It is inconsistent (and the Foreign Ministry is acutely aware of the contradiction) for Mexico to deport or mistreat Central Americans in Mexico at the same time that it complains bitterly of the treatment of undocumented Mexican workers in the United States. While the situations are not exactly parallel, Mexico loses its "moral purity" (to use the words of a Ministry official) if it restricts Central American immigration while protesting imposition of U.S. restrictions on Mexican immigration.

Although the Mexican military has been largely excluded from domestic policymaking, it is concerned with defending the integrity of Mexico's borders. The Guatemalan-Mexican border is a difficult one to patrol as most of the frontier runs through uninhabited jungle. Clearly the violation of Mexico's borders by members of Guatemala's armed forces, particularly the so-called *kaibiles* (counterinsurgency forces), is perceived as a threat and an insult by the Mexican military. The latter's task is to protect the border, and that border has been constantly violated by Guatemalan forces.

An additional security concern of the military is to prevent the spread of revolution into southern Mexico. The Central American revolutions have produced a renewed sense of mission in the military, together with a realization of the importance of putting down guerrilla movements in the Mexican countryside. Troop movements are increasing in southern Mexico and there are a greater number of military checkpoints in the border region.[33]

The Ministry of the Interior is the department of government with the most direct responsibility for the refugees. It is this department that monitors the borders and that determines not only who is allowed into the country but how long that individual may stay. Two agencies within the department are directly concerned with the refugees: Migratory Services and COMAR. Unfortunately, their goals are diametrically opposed. Of the two, Migratory Services is clearly the more powerful.

The primary responsibility of the Ministry of the Interior is maintenance of internal security. This entails both enforcing the immigration laws (including deportations) as well as ensuring political stability. Officials of this Ministry see the current dismal economic forecasts as dangerous for national security. The Ministry of the Interior, through Migratory Services, clearly, forcefully, and unambiguously advocates reducing migration into the country as a way of reducing the tensions of Mexico's beleaguered political and economic system. Ministry officials opposed moving the refugee camps away from the border for fear that such a move would make them more likely to remain in Mexico.

COMAR, on the other hand, is charged with ministering to the needs of the refugees, both through provision of economic aid and through documentation of legal appeals by refugees. While COMAR documents the appeals, however, they are made to, and decided by, Migratory Services, which serves a different set of imperatives. Luis Ortiz Monasterio, former director of COMAR under López Portillo, openly advocated a more liberal immigration policy for Central American refugees. However, COMAR is in the difficult position of being the only agency within the Mexican bureaucracy whose clientele might be considered to include the refugees. It is COMAR that administers the camps, and that works most closely with the United Nations High Commissioner for Refugees; yet, despite its good intentions, it remains a weak agency. COMAR has no budget and only a limited staff.

In addition to the institutional concerns of these relevant government agencies there are underlying political tensions that affect policymakers at all levels. Refugee policymaking is the almost exclusive domain of the executive branch and decisions on sensitive issues—such as the 1984 relocation of refugees—are made by the president himself. By and large, nongovernmental organizations have only minimal input into the policymaking process, and the Office of the UN High Commissioner for Refugees has less influence in Mexico than in any of the other countries that host large numbers of Central American refugees. Tension increased between the UNHCR and the Mexican government throughout 1983 as the latter adopted increasingly restrictive policies toward the refugees.

The politicization of refugee issues is manifest in the growing tension between state and federal authorities over who is to pay for the refugees' maintenance and by the growing involvement of religious groups in refugee issues. The religious groups have moved from provision of humanitarian aid to the refugees to advocacy in urging the adoption of more liberal asylum policies by the government.

As is the case in all Latin American countries hosting Central American refugees, personalist politics also influence the policymaking process. Policies toward refugees become identified with certain individuals within the bureaucracy. As the fortunes of these individuals rise and fall, so policies toward refugees change with them. Individuals powerful within the government are able to formulate and implement policies quite different from those enunciated at higher levels, or in other agencies. Moreover, implementation of policies in the field is dependent on functionaries who may use their position for career advancement, for personal gain, or for obtaining status and power. As in other areas, policymakers can be playing a number of different political games in the process of formulating refugee policy.

The influence of personalism in politics can manifest itself in several ways. Policies can change considerably with changes in personnel. The appointment of a new director, in Migratory Services or in COMAR, can have an impact on policies far beyond that deriving only from the individual's formal position within the bureaucracy. A case in point is that of Diana Torres, Director of Migratory Services under the López Portillo regime. She enjoyed considerable autonomy within the Ministry of the Interior, a circumstance that many suspected derived from her long-standing political relationship with the Minister of the Interior, Enrique Olivares Santana. Diana Torres represented the hard line on immigration. She viewed the influx of Central Americans into Mexico as potentially disastrous for economic and social order, and hence sought to limit migration. In line with her position, she refused to define the Central Americans as political refugees, labelling them instead as undesirable economic migrants, contributing only anarchy, crime, and promiscuity to Mexico.[34] A colorful figure, described by Excelsior columnist Manuel Buendía as "our Margaret Thatcher, the Mexican Kirkpatrick," Diana Torres did bring migration issues to public attention and took an aggressive stance in limiting the number of refugee admissions.[35]

Under the de la Madrid administration, Mario Vallejo (and his successor) have taken much more circumspect positions on refugee issues. While refusing to define the Central American immigrants as refugees, they do concede that they are motivated largely by political, not just economic, reasons. Since both individuals seem to lack the personal power of Diana Torres, they have adhered much more closely to the stated government policies and the directions of the Secretary of the Interior.

Personalist politics are also at work in field implementation of policy as well. COMAR officials have been praised for their rapid responses to mass influxes of refugees, and the generosity of individual officials has been noted by those working in the field.[36]

There have been countless charges of corruption along the border. It is widely conceded by those involved in the camps, and admitted privately by government officials, that corruption is rampant within the camps. Refugees who can pay a daily bribe to Mexican border patrols are not deported. (Even those who are deported are expected to pay the costs of their deportation.) Refugees who are employed by industrial and agricultural enterprises near the border are usually forced to work for low pay, and often required to turn over part of their daily pay to officials to prevent deportation.

Within the parameters of institutional concern, there is considerable leeway for individual government officials to maneuver, and to develop personalist policies. Decisions to clamp down or to loosen up on refugees are frequently made by individuals who act without specific instructions. This is a pattern evident throughout the region and indeed in all of the host countries examined here: personal politics have combined with national interests in shaping national refugee policies.

CONCLUSIONS

Mexico's policies toward Central American refugees can be described as ignoring them as much as possible, deporting them secretly when feasible, tolerating their presence most of the time, and discouraging more refugees from coming. The one issue on which all government and nongovernment officials agree is that a political solution to the violence provoking the flight must be achieved before there can be any answer to the dilemma that the refugees pose.

The large influx of these Central Americans into Mexico is producing a political reaction to restrict their continued immigration. A relative lack of publicity, both national and international, has enabled the Mexican government to exercise greater control over refugee admissions and to focus on national, rather than international, solutions. Mexico's increased economic difficulties have been an important factor contributing to the popular and bureaucratic pressure to limit such admissions. The pressures are apparent in the growing power of those agencies most committed to exclusion of the migrants: the Ministry of Defense and the agency of Migratory Services within the Ministry of the Interior.

Mexico's relatively closed, and highly personalist, political system contributes to this movement toward more restrictive, politicized refugee policies. The slight political opening of the system, evident in the last few years of the López Portillo regime, did lead for a time to an expansion of refugee admissions. However, the current tight economic situation has led to a corresponding tightening up of this admissions policy on the part of the de la Madrid administration. A reluctance to accept international standards of refugee definition (as exemplified by UN refugee agreements), combined with the use of refugee policy as a tool of both domestic and foreign policy, creates a highly politicized set of responses toward this situation on the part of the Mexican government. Any increase in economic, and hence political, pressure will continue to push the government toward ever more restrictive immigration policies. At the same time, Mexico's desire to achieve consistency in its policy toward Central America, while maintaining a comfortable distance from the U.S. militarism in the region, will mitigate against any outright closing of the door on the refugees.

In terms of the determinants examined here, the case of Mexican ambivalence toward the refugees seems to be explained by contradictory pressures on the policymaking process. On the most obvious level, both Mexico's foreign policy objectives and its political culture mandate more open policies toward the refugees while the government's limited capabilities—reflecting the dismal economic situation and the large numbers of Central Americans pouring across the border—limit the government's ability to respond as it would really like to. This is certainly the view that the Mexican government would like to see disseminated. And yet it is misleading in that Mexico's political commitment to the refugees is not as clear as this explanation implies. Changes in Mexican foreign policies toward Central America indicate that Mexico is perhaps less supportive of the Central American revolutions than it initially appeared. In particular, Mexico's ambivalent policies toward Guatemala have led to ambiguous policies toward the large numbers of Guatemalans seeking protection in the south.

We turn now to an examination of a case that is superficially similar to that of Mexico, a democracy with a proud heritage of political asylum and progressive foreign policies that is currently besieged with both refugees and economic difficulties: Costa Rica.

4

Costa Rica: Pressures on Neutrality

As in Mexico, the Central American refugees have poured into Costa Rica in search of safe haven. Although they have caused serious problems for the already-beleaguered Costa Rican government, Costa Rica finds itself in a very different set of political circumstances than Mexico, which affect its willingness and its capabilities of responding to the refugees.

Since 1948, Costa Rica has been held up as the shining example of democracy in Central America. While other Central American nations were mired in despotic governments, economic inequality, and social rigidity, Costa Rica was seen as in the process of constructing a just and open political system. Although somewhat idealized, this view nonetheless reflects how atypical of the region Costa Rica's development has been. Since its 1948 revolution, Costa Rica has prided itself on its commitment to democratic institutions, to a "neutral" foreign policy, and to enthusiastic support for the principles of international law and organization. The development of a welfare state at home has (at least until recently) eased social tensions and prevented violent expressions of mass discontent. However, during the past few years, profound economic problems have upset the nation's social harmony. As in the case of Mexico, Costa Rica's economic crisis has produced greater popular criticism of the government. Costa Rican foreign policies toward the United States and Central America have undergone notable shifts in the past few years as a result both of changing conditions in Central America and the worsening domestic economic situation. During the Nicaraguan insurrection of 1978-1979, Costa Rica hosted thousands of Nicaraguan refugees; after the violence subsided, most returned home. This openness to refugees was in keeping with both Costa Rican democracy and national foreign policy traditions. But as the violence in El Salvador intensified in 1980, thousands of Salvadorans began flocking to Costa Rica in search of safe haven. They were joined in 1982 by Nicaraguans fleeing the violent war with the *contras*. Since then, thousands of Nicaraguans have sought protection in Costa Rica. These large numbers of Salvadoran and Nicaraguan refugees have strained Costa Rica's ability to develop humane policies toward the refugees. Costa Rica's response to the refugees is complicated by its ambivalent policies toward the *contra* forces operating within its territory and its vacillating regional policies. As was the case in Mexico, governmental policies toward the refugees are significantly influenced by its foreign policies toward the governments of the region and toward the United States. The sections below explore Costa Rican policy toward the Central American refugees in terms of its political culture, foreign policy goals, economic conditions, and the characteristics of the refugees themselves.

A DEMOCRATIC HERITAGE

Costa Rica's democratic heritage is deeply rooted in its history.[1] During the long colonial period Costa Rica was a quiet backwater of the Spanish empire, due largely to its lack of mineral wealth and to a large indigenous population. The economy was largely based on a landholding system of small family farms. But by the mid-1800s this was being challenged by the development of coffee culture, and by the turn of the century, 5 percent of the coffee growers produced more than 50 percent of the coffee. In 1871, banana cultivation was introduced on the Atlantic Coast and blacks were imported from Louisiana and the Caribbean to build the railroads to support the largely foreign banana industry. As Barry et al. note, this phenomenon of banana cultivation gave rise to the development of two countries within Costa Rican territory: the dry, temperate coffee producing area of the Mesa Central where the capital city of San Jose is located, and the tropical, hot, banana-producing region of the Coast. The two regions developed largely in isolation from one another.[2]

The Costa Rican labor movement grew out of the struggle of the banana workers, who in the early part of the twentieth century associated with the openly-communist Bloque de Obreros y Campesinos. This organization (which later changed its name to the Vanguardia) was very successful in organizing the banana workers. While the workers were organizing a progressive movement on the coast, Costa Rican politics in the central highlands were developing in a more traditional fashion. Although relatively free elections were held in 1899 and the trappings of democracy were maintained through most of the period, by 1948 domination by an elite class characterized political life. The political system was under considerable strain owing to the growing literacy of the population and increasing demands for political participation, at the same time that radical movements were emerging from the workers' organizations. Pressure was building to break the domination of the elite, but at the same time splits were developing within the opposition movement.

In 1942 rising young politician José Figueres Ferrer denounced the power of the Vanguardia forces, creating a schism between the so-called "moderate" reformers and the more progressive leftist forces. In a move that would have significance thirty years later for the development of Costa Rican policies toward the refugees, José Figueres went into exile. From there he received arms and military aid in exchange for the promise that once successful, he would help exile groups working in Nicaragua and the Dominican Republic. Thus from the very beginning, Figueres linked his rule with support for revolutionary forces elsewhere.

In the 1948 elections, the incumbent National Republicans manipulated the results, claimed victory, and refused to give up power. Figueres entered Costa Rica with his troops and allies from Guatemala, and fought a civil war that lasted six weeks and resulted in 7,000 deaths. The Costa Rican democracy that was established through that revolution was thus the product of dissidents who had organized outside the country and were supplied with foreign arms. The political system that emerged also reflected the splits between the opposition forces. When besieged by Figueres' forces, the government of the National Republicans requested assistance from the Vanguardia forces to prevent Figueres from attaining power. As in the case of the Mexican revolution, U.S. intervention played a crucial role at a decisive moment in the revolution. As the revolution assumed the character of a three-way struggle between Figueres, the incumbent National Republicans, and the Vanguardia, the U.S. government delivered an ultimatum, saying that it would intervene if Figueres did not attain power. Figueres and the Vanguardia worked out a compromise; the pact between the two forces reflected a major concession to the Vanguardia in its inclusion of social legislation and support for workers' rights.

In many ways, the Costa Rican revolution parallels the Mexican case. In both countries the struggle against the elitist status quo was a military one and in both cases the more radical forces were either militarily defeated or coopted by the more moderate victors. U.S. force, either through military pressure (Mexico) or threats (Costa Rica), was instrumental in securing the victory of the moderate forces. But while the Mexican government developed in a more authoritarian fashion and with much more (at least rhetorical) commitment to radical social change,

Figueres moved to consolidate democratic political institutions in a much more moderate fashion.

The democracy that Figueres was able to establish in Costa Rica is without parallel in Central America. By and large, the democratic institutions function well. The constitution created a unitary system with a strong central government and a relatively weak president (and in 1969, a further restriction was added, limiting presidential tenure to a single four year term). Governmental ministers, although appointed and dismissed by the president, enjoy considerable autonomy. The unicameral legislative assembly is the strongest branch of government in the country with the power to summon ministers and override the veto. Multiple checks and balances in the system are designed to prevent the abuses of power so common elsewhere.

The PLN (Partido de Liberación Nacional), the vehicle created by José (Pepe) Figueres, is the oldest continuous party in the country and has become closely identified with the existing system of government. In 1968, the more radical members of the PLN tried to move the party in a more leftist direction but "Don Pepe" threatened to withdraw from the PLN and create a new party if the radicals won. His pressure was successful in holding the party together. In July 1976, Figueres precipitated a crisis within the party leadership by calling for reform of the constitutional requirement that a president may not serve two successive terms and subsequently resigned his post as party chairman. Because of the dominance of the PLN and the constitutional requirement that a successful presidential candidate receive 40 percent of the vote in order to be elected, opposition parties frequently resort to coalition politics. In 1978, Rodrigo Carazo was elected president on the Unitary Party ticket after splitting off from the PLN. But the Unitary Coalition fell apart in the wake of economic problems, difficulties in foreign policy, and charges of corruption; and in 1982, Luis Alberto Monge of the PLN won the election with almost 60 percent of the vote.

One of the most persistent problems facing the Costa Rican democracy is the growing cost of the welfare state. Since its 1948 revolution, the Costa Rican government has devoted extraordinary resources to education and social services. A comprehensive package of social benefits —from unemployment insurance to the Costa Rican equivalent of food stamps—is available to Costa Rican citizens. The results of this financial commitment have been impressive. Costa Rican literacy rates and health indicators are not only the highest in Central America, but rank among the best in the Third World. Yet the welfare state has created both political and economic problems for the government. Twenty percent of the population work in the state sector[3] and, as discussed below, this has created serious economic problems that limit the government's room for independent action.

Costa Rica's political culture includes a strong commitment to democratic institutions and to the principles of international law and organization. Furthermore, as the product of a revolution launched from the territory of a neighboring country, Costa Rica has traditionally served as a refuge for Latin American political dissidents. Costa Rica played a vital role in the Nicaraguan revolution by providing sanctuary to 70,000 to 100,000 Nicaraguan refugees during the war and by permitting the Sandinista leadership to carry out operations from Costa Rican territory. Without this support, the Nicaraguan revolutionaries would have had a much more difficult time in actually succeeding in their revolutionary drive.

By virtue of its political traditions, proud heritage of democracy, and past actions, the Costa Rican government was clearly predisposed to adopt generous policies toward individuals fleeing repressive governments. Yet, as discussed below, by 1980 harsh economic realities combined with a lessening of the nation's traditional neutrality began to pose limits to these good intentions.

In spite of the existence of smoothly-functioning democratic institutions Costa Rica currently faces serious political problems. There are still grave inequities in land tenure and a powerful elite still dominates much of the nation's political life. Although opposition parties are free to organize and campaign (and historically have done very poorly at the polls), the combination of difficult domestic economic conditions and a widening war in Central America are seen as threatening to the nation's stability. Beginning in 1980, there was a sudden surge in political violence. In the space of 23 months, there were 14 violent incidents, an unprecedented number for Costa Rica. However, only four of those incidents—two shootouts, a bombing, and an assault on U.S. embassy guards en route to their posts—were carried out by Costa Ricans (and even then by members of a very small group). The others were all the result of intrigues by foreigners—Nicaraguans, Salvadorans, Hondurans, Guatemalans, Argentinians, Chileans, and perhaps Uruguayans.[4] This fear of becoming a battleground for foreigners has become a very important component of current Costa Rican foreign policy.

VACILLATING NEUTRALITY

Since 1948, Costa Rica's foreign policy has been based on close ties with the United States, support for other democratic regimes, and a commitment to international law and organization. Like other small nations,

Costa Rica has seen the United Nations as a means of providing for its national security as well as aiding the creation of a more just international order. Together with its democratic institutions and foreign policy tradition of "neutrality," Costa Rica has actively promoted the development of global political institutions. Thus, Costa Rica is a party to the relevant international conventions on refugees and feels bound by these international commitments. Following his victory in 1948, President Figueres officially abolished the military, heralding an important new era in Costa Rican domestic and foreign politics. Although there are armed police forces in the country—forces that are growing in sophistication and importance, given events in the region—Costa Rica is very proud of its rejection of military force in foreign policy. The lack of a military has meant more resources available for social programs, lack of a military alternative when political conditions deteriorate, and a greater commitment to nonviolent resolution of conflicts. The country's security forces are under firm civilian control. In fact, both the Civil Guard (under the Ministry of Public Service) and the Rural Guard (under the Ministry of the Interior) are politically appointed and completely replaced with each administration. Thus, each new presidential administration fills some 8,000 positions in the Guard. This ensures that there will be no continuity of leadership and prevents the army from playing an important role in Costa Rican politics.[5] This has also been an area of U.S. pressure on the Costa Rican government, as the United States feels that a strong Costa Rican military is essential for regional security.

Costa Rican relations with the United States have been generally quite good since 1948. Pepe Figueres always had very close connections with U.S. politicians, including admitted contacts with the CIA. As J. Kenen put it, Costa Rica has a symbiotic relationship with the United States.[6] Washington wants a showplace democracy in Central America and support for its current policies in the region, while Costa Rica wants investment and aid from the United States. Costa Rican industrialization in the 1960s was largely the product of U.S. investors. Yet while Costa Rica is economically dependent on the United States and acutely aware of this dependence in the present period of huge national debts, Costa Ricans are at the same time somewhat uneasy at thoughts of too close a relationship. As in the case of Mexico, this uneasy dependence on the United States acts as a constant pressure on Costa Rica's foreign policies toward the Central American region.

Historically, Costa Rica has considered itself somewhat apart from the other Central American republics. Politically, it differed from the pattern of authoritarian governments and economically its higher standard of living and commitment to social welfare policies set it apart from the more rigid governments of the region. Relations with Central

American nations have not been given nearly as much emphasis as ties with the United States.

Costa Rican foreign policy toward Central America is also shaped by a legacy of troubled relations with Nicaragua. From the very beginning of their existence as independent nations, Costa Rica and Nicaragua have been in conflict. Costa Rican occupation of the Nicaraguan province of Nicoya in 1824 and continual disputes over the San Juan River almost erupted in war. In 1858, the Cañas Jerez Treaty gave Nicaragua full sovereignty over the river with the provision that Costa Rica would have the perpetual right of free navigation, which could not be hindered even in the event of war. The issue of navigation rights arose in 1977 and 1978 when Somoza's National Guard fired on Costa Rican ships on the river. Currently relations between the Sandinista and the Monge governments have been strained over issues of Sandinista security measures along the San Juan river, which Costa Rica sees as an infringement of the treaty.

While Costa Rica was one of the most important supporters of the Nicaraguan insurrection, relations have sharply deteriorated since the Sandinista victory in 1979. In a well-reasoned essay, R. D. Tomasek explores the reasons for the breakdown in relations as follows. First, Costa Rican leaders and the populace have become disenchanted with the way Nicaragua's political system has emerged. Costa Rican leaders expected the emergence of pluralism in Nicaragua; they have become very disillusioned with the postponing of democracy. Tomasek reports that "[I]n 1981 *La Nación* published a secret speech by Humberto Ortega in which he maintained that Costa Rican 'bourgeois' democracy was not suitable for Nicaragua and that popular power as defended by the leaders was a truer type of democracy."[7]

Another serious point of contention between the two governments concerns Costa Rica's toleration and alleged support of *contra* forces, who conduct military operations against the Nicaraguan government from Costa Rican territory. The Costa Rican government maintains that it is simply trying to apply its policy on asylum to the exile groups. As discussed below, the operation of various Nicaraguan exile groups, notably ARDE (Alianza Revolucionaria Democrática) under the leadership of Eden Pastora and Alfonso Robelo, has been a growing source of harassment for the Nicaraguan government. A more fundamental problem for Costa Rica is that it cannot control its own border. The Costa Rican-Nicaraguan border is 220 miles long and located in deep jungle with virtually no roads. Only 300–500 Civil Guards are stationed along the border, although more are called in when sweeps occur. The sweeps of the area are largely ineffective because of their widely publicized nature, the camps' locations, and widespread popular support for Pastora. Costa Rica's inability to prevent Nicaraguan exile groups from using its territory also means that refugees as well as *contras* cannot be prevented from entering.

The Central American violence impinges on Costa Rica in other ways as well. There is a strong belief among Costa Rican leaders—a belief that seems to be supported by the general public—that Nicaragua (and Cuba) are involved in efforts to overthrow the Costa Rican government and to discredit it in international public opinion. Given the economic difficulties facing the country, and current public unrest, Costa Rican leaders feel insecure in their own political positions. They see international provocateurs as responsible for many of their domestic difficulties. The Costa Rican Office of Judicial Investigation has described a plan through which a thousand Costa Ricans—many trained in Cuba and Nicaragua—are planning to foment strikes and infiltrate organizations as a means of subverting the government.[8] These sorts of accusations play on national anti-Nicaraguan sentiment and serve to divert attention and criticism from national political leaders. Given the dismal state of the Costa Rican economy, it is useful for Costa Rican officials to accuse foreign agents of exacerbating local conditions.

Costa Rica's economic crisis has forced the government to seek aid from the IMF and from the U.S. government. These efforts by the government to move closer to the U.S. are derided in Nicaragua as evidence of Costa Rican submission to U.S. pressure. Thus in December 1982, the Nicaraguan government published a full-page statement in Costa Rican newspapers asserting that Costa Rican president Monge's trip to Washington in search of economic aid was an extreme case of submissiveness. Costa Rican officials were so indignant that they sent a diplomatic protest note to Nicaraguan authorities.[9] Charges that Costa Rica is a powerless client of the United States perhaps hit too close to home to be tolerated.

Relations between the Costa Rican government, Nicaragua, and the United States have reflected an uneasy and vacillating balance between conflicting foreign policy objectives. On the one hand, the Costa Rican government fears the spillover of revolutionary violence into Costa Rica (particularly given the nation's serious economic conditions) and distrusts the Sandinista government. On the other hand, Costa Rican governments are leery of too close an alignment with the United States, particularly in supporting repressive governments in the other Central American countries. These contradictory foreign policy pressures are all played out against a backdrop of a traditional support for neutrality.

The 1982 election of Luis Alberto Monge seemed to indicate a shift toward a policy of closer alignment with the United States in opposing the Sandinista regime. Thus in his first visit to Washington, Monge affirmed that Nicaragua "is converting itself into a totalitarian dictatorship with the strong support of Cuba."[10] Costa Rican diplomatic initiatives in the region were designed to contain Nicaraguan influence. For example, in October 1982, Foreign Minister Volio set up a "Forum for Peace and Democracy," which included a role for the United States as observer while excluding Nicaragua and Guatemala. Colombia and Panama subsequently withdrew to join the Contadora Group begun by Mexico and Venezuela, and by February 1983, only Costa Rica, Honduras, and El Salvador remained as Central American members. Monge publicly admitted that U.S. presence in the group was a reason for its failure.[11] On November 17, 1983, Monge officially proclaimed Costa Rica's neutrality, setting off a loud public debate on the subject. The neutrality statute stipulates that Costa Rica "has no military, will not build a military, will not go to war with any other state, will not participate in any wars in Central America, will not interfere in the domestic affairs of any other country, and expects that other states will reciprocate by not interfering in Costa Rican internal affairs."[12] This declaration on neutrality is intended to become part of the Costa Rican constitution through amendment. U.S. support for this declaration of neutrality was unenthusiastic; in fact the United States criticized the statement on neutrality as endangering U.S. support for Costa Rica and the nation's defense against the Nicaraguan government.[13]

Neutrality has been a fundamental component of Costa Rican foreign policy since 1948; Costa Rican leaders have consistently appealed to the ideal of neutrality in developing their foreign policy positions. As J. K. Lincoln explains, historically neutrality has meant avoidance of "entangling alliances."[14] It has also served as a means for limiting U.S. influence in the country and for limiting conflict among PLN party leaders. The deliberate and conscious removal of a military option and the broad consensus for a neutral stance has served to unify national leaders in foreign policy issues.

But Costa Rican neutrality has never been absolute; in fact it has been remarkably flexible, as witnessed in Costa Rica's open support for the Nicaraguan insurrectionists. By the end of that war, the Costa Rican government was officially allowing planes to land on Costa Rican soil with arms for the revolutionaries. J.K. Lincoln describes Costa Rica's current policy of neutrality as "an active neutrality" in which the government supports diplomatic efforts to protect its national security and to deal with the region's crises through 1) the Contadora Group's negotiations, 2) direct negotiations between the Salvadoran guerrillas and the government of that country, and 3) unilateral efforts on the part of the United States.[15] In essence, the Costa Rican government is trying to maintain some distance from the Central American violence, to appease nationalistic pressures opposing a more pro-U.S. policy, and to respond to the obvious preferences of the regional powers making up the Contadora Group.

But it became increasingly difficult for the Costa Rican government to maintain a position of "active neutrality" in light of continued U.S. pressures on Costa Rica to develop military forces to respond to the Sandinista military buildup. U.S. pressure on Costa Rica has been unrelenting and has been particularly focused on building up Costa Rica's military forces. In September 1983 the U.S. representative to the United Nations warned Costa Rica that its economic aid would be reduced if it did not build up an army.[16] In November of 1983 the U.S. government offered 1,000 men from the U.S. Corps of Engineers to build up Costa Rican roads and infrastructure along the Nicaraguan border.[17] In the face of this U.S. pressure, the Costa Rican government has vacillated in its foreign policies. Personnel changes, ambivalent policies toward the *contras,* and contradictory governmental statements indicate often confused governmental intentions in the region.[18]

Contradictions and pressures on Costa Rica's neutrality have been increasingly evident as ARDE (Alianza Revolucionaria Democrática) forces led by Eden Pastora have been using Costa Rican territory as a staging ground for its military operations against the Sandinista regime. Eden Pastora was a popular figure in Costa Rica during the Sandinistas' long struggle against Somoza, and given Costa Rican suspicions about the revolutionary regime in Nicaragua, he received considerable support from the Costa Rican population. On the other hand, ARDE's activities clearly violated the nation's neutrality and drew Costa Rica more deeply into the region's violence. Conditions became so tense along the border that in May 1983, the Costa Rican government asked the Contadora Group to place an observation team on the border. Even though the Costa Rican government has occasionally expelled Eden Pastora, the ARDE leader has been permitted to return to the country. In a visit to the United States in December 1983, President Monge stated that he could not seek a complete expulsion of anti-Sandinista forces "since to do so would violate their right to political asylum."[19] As violence in the northern region has accelerated and as border incidents have increased, the dangers to Costa Rican stability of tolerating the continued use of its territory for anti-Nicaraguan activities have also grown.

There is a substantial and very real fear in Costa Rica of the effects of the spillover of revolutionary violence. A widely-expressed concern in Costa Rica is that San José is becoming a center for international espionage. The *contras* seem to operate in San José with the implicit approval, or at least the studied indifference, of the government. In spite of governmental statements of neutrality, permitting the *contra* forces to launch military attacks against a neighboring country is clearly a very political act.

Costa Rican policies in the region are further characterized by their lack of consistency. While the Monge government appears to support a "two track" policy of support for both diplomatic negotiations and increasing alignment with the United States, there are splits within the government. J. K. Lincoln reports that the Minister of Gobernación "who commands the Rural Guard and the Minister of Public Security, who commands the Civil Guard, have openly disagreed about a proper governmental response to Pastora's operations in the north."[20] Monge moved to support the latter's contention that Pastora's operations threatened Costa Rica's neutrality.

By early 1984, Costa Rica seemed to be moving toward a more openly pro-U.S. policy. Costa Rica will receive over $18 million in the next two years in military assistance from the United States to improve the level of professionalization of its Civil Guard. Military assistance from the United States to Costa Rica increased from $3 million in 1983 to $9 million in 1984 and 1985 and was to be used for communications, transportation, and weapons. The United States is also preparing to train a Civil Guard battalion, which will be called a "Reaction Force for Costa Rica" and comprised of four independent companies of approximately 180 men each. Lincoln reports that one of the invisible strings attached to this aid is that the officers of these battalions should remain through changes in administration. Such a condition will make it more difficult for Costa Rica to claim that it has no standing army.[21]

There has been considerable domestic opposition over these close ties with the United States. In May 1984, former Costa Rican presidents Oduber and Figueres marched with 20,000 demonstrators against the policies of war and intervention in the region, and the PLN candidate supports neutrality. On the other hand, the presidential candidate of the opposition PUSC (Social Christian Unity Party) has said that his first act as president would be to eliminate the word "neutrality" from the Costa Rican vocabulary.

The economic crisis facing the Costa Rican government has undoubtedly contributed to its vacillating foreign policies. Clearly the government needed U.S. support in renegotiating its debt. Genuine concerns about the nation's security, given the Nicaraguan buildup, together with economic needs led the Monge government to support U.S. initiatives in the region. At the same time, however, traditional Costa Rican traditions of neutrality and some popular resentment against the government's activist policies mitigated against being drawn too deeply into the conflict on the side of the United States. Most of all, the Costa Rican government has tried to keep the region's violence and chaos out of their nation. The economic instability and the growing political discontent have produced a volatile domestic situation and for the first time knowledgeable observers have begun talking of a possible "Uruguayization" of the country—referring to the pattern in Uruguay where economic decline in the 1960s was used to justify a military takeover in the 1970s.[22]

Costa Rica's foreign policy interests have created contradictory pressures in responding to the needs of the Central American refugees seeking protection within its borders. While its political culture mandates acceptance of the refugees in accord with international law and its domestic heritage of freedom for political dissidents, at the same time, conflicts with Nicaragua and ambivalent support for U.S. objectives in the region serve to temper that support. The conflicts with Nicaragua have created a predisposition toward generous policies toward the Nicaraguan refugees. Yet support for the U.S. position in the region and a fear of the spreading of the violence from El Salvador to Costa Rica creates a predisposition to be much less generous toward the Salvadorans seeking refuge from the violence. Against this backdrop of substantial domestic political unrest and contradictions in Costa Rican foreign policy, the question of the economic crisis has taken on a new urgency.

THE DETERIORATING ECONOMY

Traditionally the Costa Rican economy has been characterized by its small size and its openness to foreign investment. Indeed C. Gonzalez-Vega notes that Costa Rica has one of the most open economies in the world. During the 1960s, the Costa Rican economy went through a period of expansion. Both industrial development and exports of agricultural products grew at impressive rates. Between 1960 and 1980, Costa Rica's GDP grew at an average rate of 5.8 percent per year. But this average concealed some important differences in growth rates over time—the growth rate during 1965–1970 was 7 percent; during 1970–1975, 6.0 percent; and during 1975–1980, 5.2 percent[23]—as well as some serious structural problems. In a pattern common throughout the Third World, as exports of agricultural luxuries (for example, flowers, strawberries) to the United States increased, landlessness among peasants also grew. As J. Kenen points out, the "white legend" of Costa Rica—the long-standing belief in peace and democracy—obscured the reality of grave inequalities in land distribution and the concentration of power in the hands of a few.[24] Indeed, by the late 1960s nearly three-quarters of Costa Rica's peasants were landless.

This openness of the economy and reliance on exports of agricultural products created a situation where external events have had a major impact on the country's economic well-being. The international oil crises of 1973 and 1978, the steep decline in the international prices for agricultural products, and changes in Costa Rica's access to international credit created a situation of virtual economic dependency. Barry et al. report that the fall in coffee prices was particularly acute. The value of Costa Rica's 1980 exports could buy only 76 percent of the imports that they could buy in 1977.[25] Strikes increased rapidly and for the first time a guerrilla movement appeared in 1980. The lack of resources meant that the elites were unable to "buy off" the peasants.

During the past five years, the economic crisis has deepened, directly affecting the government's political popularity and the foreign economic policy orientation of the regime. In 1981, the country's GNP experienced a decline of 3.6 percent, inflation was running at 54 percent annually, and rising oil prices and falling coffee production had led to a $300 million deficit in national reserves. In 1982 the GDP fell by 9.1 percent.[26] The government was unable to pay the service on its $4 billion external debt. In fact, the government was in an impossible bind. The government had no foreign currency reserves, no prospects for new loans, and was faced with the depressing prospect of negotiating with the International Monetary Fund.[27] This crisis was symptomatic of deeper structural problems in the Costa Rican economy.

Monge sought to implement a number of economic policies including development of natural resources in agriculture, mining, and fishing, attracting private and international investment in agribusiness, land reform, and support for the Central American Common Market. But Monge's first task and the one that clearly dominated his agenda was responding to the IMF.

Negotiations with the IMF were painful. In 1982, the central bank cut subsidies on utilities and fuel, raised taxes, and froze wages to reduce its public sector deficit. In October, the IMF agreed to a $100 million standby credit in exchange for low public sector borrowing, a wage freeze, and higher fuel and electricity prices.[28] These measures directly affected the poorest sectors and resulted in rising crime rates, violent protests against the government, and splits within the PLN itself over economic policy. In fact, the economic figures for 1982 could hardly have been more depressing: inflation reached 90 percent, the GDP declined by 6 percent (although some estimates put the decline at 9.1 percent), exports declined by 15 percent, and the world prices of both coffee and sugar fell.[29]

In 1983, the political situation deteriorated as the impact of the stringent IMF terms began to be felt. In April 1983 teachers went on strike and banana workers protested the practice of companies laying off workers by switching from banana growing to palm oil production. Unions protested these actions and efforts by banana transnationals to push for a 40 percent cut on export duties.[30] During the six week strike by workers of the Costa Rican Banana Company—a subsidiary of United Brands—Costa Rica lost $700,000 in lost wages, $12 million in lost production, and $500,000 in export taxes. Soon after the strike was settled, United Brands announced that it was closing the company and ending operations in Costa Rica. This move will idle 3,000 workers and create a loss in exports of $37.5 million. A general agricultural problem arose when squatters began occupying banana growing areas. The government implemented an emergency land reform program, but this action was not enough to quell the unrest.[31]

At the same time, Monge continued his negotiations with the IMF and finally an agreement was signed in September 1983, providing for additional loan guarantees in return for compliance with specific economic policies. But as the standard of living for the workers continued to fall, political unrest increased. By 1983, 71 percent of all Costa Ricans were living below the government defined "poverty line"—even though as recently as 1977 the figure was only 24 percent.[32]

Continued negotiations with the IMF resulted in the announcement of a letter of intent in mid-1984. By August the banana workers' strike had ended. The economic crisis provoked a major political upheaval, however; coup rumors were rampant in San José and PLN popularity fell to a new low. Monge reshuffled his cabinet.

The economic difficulties experienced by Costa Rica had several effects on Costa Rican receptivity to Central American refugees. Most obviously, they decreased the resources available to the government to respond to the needs of refugees. During a period of scarcity, when the standard of living of the Costa Rican populace was falling, foreigners were greeted with suspicion, particularly when they came across in great numbers. Furthermore, Costa Rica's precarious economic position put pressure on the government vis à vis the United States. Costa Rica needed U.S. support to extricate itself from a difficult economic situation. One of the most striking examples of the way in which Costa Rica's urgent economic needs influenced its policy of neutrality and its policies toward Central America occurred in 1984. As J. K. Lincoln reports, in the summer of 1984 the EEC foreign ministers met with Central American foreign ministers in San José and promised to increase aid to the region from $40 million to $53 million annually. Costa Rica's participation in this group was clearly a response to a desire for more multilateral relations in the region. Yet, with many of these foreign ministers still in town, Monge met with U.S. Ambassador Curtis Winsor, who promised that the United States would give an additional $60 million to Costa Rica alone.[33]

Costa Rica's economic situation has thus directly affected both its foreign policy and the domestic political situation. In this context, the arrival of large numbers of Central American refugees made the contradictions even more apparent.

THE CENTRAL AMERICAN REFUGEES IN COSTA RICA

As mentioned above, during the Nicaraguan civil war between 70,000 and 90,000 Nicaraguans sought temporary refuge on Costa Rican territory. During the insurrection the Costa Rican government supported the Nicaraguan revolutionaries quite openly, even breaking relations with the Somoza regime. Clearly, however, the Costa Rican government hoped for a more moderate regime. Following the revolution, all but 20,000 Nicaraguans returned to Nicaragua.

Then in early 1980 Salvadoran refugees began arriving. By 1982 the UNHCR representative in Costa Rica reported that 10,000 Salvadorans were in the country (as well as 200 Guatemalans, 2,000 Cubans awaiting U.S. processing, 2,000 Nicaraguans, and a smaller number of South Americans and Haitians).[34] As conditions in El Salvador worsened, the refugee flow increased.

The response of the Costa Rican government and the United Nations High Commissioner for Refugees (UNHCR) in Costa Rica to the Salvadoran refugees has been very positive, at least for those Salvadorans formally recognized by the government. The Salvadorans are granted formal refugee status and are deemed eligible for a wide range of economic and social benefits. Emergency assistance for the refugees began in 1980 with an initial caseload of 2,500 Salvadoran refugees, mostly in urban areas, especially San José. At first, around 200 lived in tents while the rest rented modest rooms in the capital. By January 1981, 6,500 refugees were living in the central plateau, primarily in San José. By 1984, the UNHCR estimated a total of 15,000 Salvadoran refugees were in the country, but some private estimates are much higher, up to 90,000 to 100,000.[35] (There is a clear incentive for the Salvadoran government and the UNHCR to underestimate the Salvadoran refugees in order to avoid having to provide aid and jobs to foreigners in light of current economic difficulties.)

The Los Angeles farm, in Guanacaste, was created as a model farm for an initial group of 216 Salvadoran refugees who were given asylum by the Costa Rican government after an incident in which they occupied the Costa Rican embassy in El Salvador. The 191 hectare farm, constructed at a cost of $1.14 million and intended for 500 people, now houses 350-400 Salvadoran refugees.[36] It serves the needs of only a very few of the thousands of refugees in the country and is generally not regarded as successful, much less as a model. The high cost of the farm, the relatively small number of refugees living in Los Angeles, and perhaps the fact that most of those originally settled in Los Angeles were a group of very politicized Salvadorans who had seized the Costa Rican embassy in El Salvador, have contributed to its difficulties. Indeed, one UNHCR official in Costa Rica contends that the main problem with the settlement has been the unsuitable nature of the initial group of refugees.

The majority of Salvadorans live in San José, where 6,500 Salvadorans are given daily food rations, medical assistance, housing allowance, and daycare centers. However, there are many Salvadorans living in urban areas without any international assistance. Most of the Salvadoran refugees who make it to Costa Rica have come from urban areas, as Salvadoran peasants are much more likely to seek refuge in either Salvadoran cities or across the border in Honduras. Thus, rural resettlement schemes are not particularly attractive alternatives for the Salvadorans who come.

UNHCR's financial crisis in 1985 led the organization to begin the phase-out of emergency assistance to Salvadoran refugees in Costa Rica. The elimination of the subsidies will be particularly painful in light of the fact that most of these refugees are not legally entitled to work. It seems unlikely that either the Costa Rican government or the nongovernmental organization will be able to compensate for UNHCR's cutbacks.

A second group of refugees who began arriving in Costa Rica during 1982/83 are Nicaraguans who are either disaffected with the revolutionary government or who have been caught in the crossfire between the *contra* forces operating out of Costa Rica and the Nicaraguan government. One U.S. government official estimated that 80 percent of the Nicaraguans who come are victims of ARDE military operations. In response to the flow of Nicaraguans, the Costa Rican government initially opened two reception centers. One of these is in Limón, on the Atlantic coast; it houses approximately 250-300 Nicaraguans, many of whom are Nicaraguan Miskitus and have some cultural affinity with coastal residents in Costa Rica. A second camp was opened at Tilarán, in Guanacaste. Tilarán was the former camp for hundreds of workers constructing a major hydroelectric facility. Its dormitories, shops, and recreation areas have served the needs of the refugees fairly well, although its intended capacity of 1,000 has been strained by the presence of 2,100 Nicaraguans. However, by international standards of refugee camps, the Tilarán inhabitants are relatively well off.

Although the government officially acknowledges those Nicaraguans living in camps as refugees, thousands more Nicaraguans live in the country without official government sanction. As most of the border runs through dense jungle and is unpatrolled by Costa Rican security forces, it is relatively easy for Nicaraguans to enter the country undetected by Costa Rican authorities. Moreover, as one Costa Rican official said, "even if we could effectively patrol the border, how can we stop them from coming across? We can't just shoot women and children, even if we can detain them." Another government official likened the Costa Rican border to a sponge in which tens of thousands of Nicaraguan migrants are simply soaked up. Many Nicaraguans are leaving their country to avoid the draft and whole families have moved into Costa Rican cities. Officials report that private school enrollment figures are up. While publicly officials report that there are approximately 15,000 Nicaraguan refugees in the country, privately the same officials refer to 90,000 Nicaraguans.[37]

The 90,000 Nicaraguans and 90,000 Salvadorans together create an almost unbearably high percentage of refugees in the general population; in fact, if these figures are close to being accurate, approximately one in ten people residing within Costa Rica's national territory is a refugee. The demands such numbers place on an already overburdened government are enormous.

COSTA RICA'S POLICIES TOWARD THE REFUGEES

To coordinate the needs of the refugees the National Commission for Refugees (COMPARE) was formed in 1980, with representatives of the ministries of Security, Gobernación, Foreign Relations, Planning, Labor, and Justice, as well as the Red Cross, IMAS (Joint Institute of Social Assistance), and IMA (Instituto Nacional de Aprendizaje). In January of 1984 the structure was reorganized into three groups: 1) a commission made up of the ministers or vice-ministers of Justice, Security, Gobernación, IMAS, ICM (Intergovernmental Committee for Migration), and UNHCR (the latter with a voice but no vote) that meets weekly to set general policies; 2) the Comité de Programas y Proyectos made up of representatives of the same ministries, who study and coordinate the various programs and agencies working in the country (this committee meets weekly with clear operational responsibilities); and 3) an emergency committee to respond rapidly to the cases requiring rapid attention.

Unlike the case in all other host countries, the head of COMPARE and the individual charged with coordinating national refugee policies is the Minister of Justice. The reason for this seems largely due to individual factors. In 1979 Justice Minister Elizabeth Odio Benito was deeply committed to providing for the Nicaraguan refugees, and in the absence of strong pressure from the Foreign Minister she emerged as a natural choice for the position. Under Monge's administration, the Justice Minister has continued to play the crucial role in coordinating national refugee policies. The fact that it is the Justice Ministry that provides this coordinating role is a reflection of the governmental belief that refugee issues are primarily to be dealt with as a legal obligation of the Costa Rican government.

There is also a wide range of private organizations who are involved in refugee relief. Caritas, for example, is active in urban areas and is in charge of all small business projects. The refugees' right to work is limited to self-sufficiency projects financed by the UNHCR. This limitation was designed to prevent undue competition with unemployed Costa Ricans, but creates a climate of dependency on government aid. One of the main employment problems faced by the refugees is that many, perhaps most, are illiterate, while among Costa Ricans the literacy rate is approximately 90 percent, making it difficult for refugees to compete in the job market.

Refugee issues in Costa Rica are very politicized and several inter-related conflicts can be identified: growing xenophobia among the Costa Rican population, differences in Costa Rican perceptions of Salvadorans and Nicaraguans, and difficult relations between the UNHCR and the Costa Rican government. The increasing violence in El Salvador and the growing intensity of the *contra* attacks against Nicaragua have also contributed to a growing desire to distance the nation from the region's troubles. At present feelings are running very high in Costa Rica, particularly anti-Sandinista feelings. In response to both popular senti-ments and to the economic and political problems facing the government, the government is becoming more restrictive toward Central American migrants of all kinds. In December 1982, President Monge and the Minister of the Interior Alfonso Carro signed into a law a regulation requiring Salvadorans and Nicaraguans entering the country to have both a passport (or equivalent documents) and a visa issued by Costa Rican authorities in the country-of-origin, as well as return passage. [38] Yet in 1984, thousands of Nicaraguans were still crossing daily into Costa Rica without such documents, and although they were not given permission to work in the country, they were not denied entry.

The anti-foreign attitudes exhibited by Costa Ricans stem from both the economic conditions of the country and the feeling that the nation has lost control of its own borders. The lack of available land for needy Costa Rican families makes it difficult for the government to be generous in providing land for foreign refugees. With growing landlessness among Costa Rican peasants, it is politically impossible for the govern-ment to give land to refugees. In this context of limited economic resources, the efforts of the government to develop "durable solutions" to deal with the refugees are certainly admirable from a humanitarian standpoint. As one COMPARE official stated, "We have a responsibility to help train the refugees as much as possible while they're here. If they stay in the country for a long period, they will be more likely to contribute to the nation's well-being than if they had been idly sitting in camps. And if they return home, they'll be better able to help their home countries." However, such projects—when designed exclusively for refugees—inevitably produce resentment on the part of Costa Ricans. As another official said, "presently there are almost 150 projects underway for refugees and they have almost all failed. Virtually, every project designed strictly for foreigners has failed while those that have been successful have incorporated both Costa Ricans and refugees."

Officials in government agencies charged with caring for the refugees, as well as Costa Ricans generally, see the refugees' presence as having contributed to rising crime rates in the country. As one government official explained, "since Nicaraguans entering the country after January 1983 are not allowed to work and since they have a real need to support their families, they turn to crime."

While Costa Ricans have generally been sympathetic toward Nicaraguans leaving their country in the past few years, there is growing resentment and suspicion of Salvadoran migrants. Representative of this view were the opinions of one Costa Rican official involved with refugee relief. He explained that the Salvadorans who come are "all Communists." When asked "then why don't they stay in Nicaragua?" the official explained that they really weren't refugees; rather "they are communists infiltrating the country to cause internal dissent and eventual revolution." The perception that the Salvadorans are communist agents, troublemakers, and present in the country in order to cause problems for the government is widespread among both Costa Rican officials and the general population. While the Nicaraguans are viewed with more sympathy for leaving their country because of Sandinista actions, traditional rivalries between Nicaragua and Costa Rica, together with the pressures generated by the dismal economic situation, have limited Costa Rican welcome of Nicaraguan refugees.

Relations between the UNHCR and the Costa Rican government have at times been tense. There have been conflicts over the extent to which the UNHCR should exercise power over the refugees. As an official of a government agency involved in providing direct relief to the refugees explains, "UNHCR comes in with their money and their international standards and tries to tell us how to give welfare to the refugees. But we know what problems can be caused in such a fashion. When a refugee lines up at a window at IMAS and receives 1,000 colones or 3,000 colones while right next to him a poor Costa Rican only receives 100 colones, resentment grows and aid for refugees is endangered."

The UNHCR's efforts to control operations within the camps to ensure implementation of certain policies are also resented by some government officials. Efforts by the Costa Rican government to limit the UNHCR's authority have been resisted by the UNHCR. There is a widespread perception in the Costa Rican government that the UNHCR prefers the Salvadorans to the Nicaraguan refugees. One official privately accused the UNHCR of funnelling money to the Salvadoran guerrillas through the Los Angeles camp. The camp itself is somewhat controversial as it represents a substantial investment for a relatively few refugees.

One of the most serious points of controversy between the Costa Rican government and the UNHCR is over the location of future camps. The present camps are clearly inadequate for the number of refugees coming across the border. The Costa Rican government leased, with an option to buy, land in Rio Claro for an additional refugee camp. The site, near the Panamanian border, was opposed by the UNHCR on grounds that it is located near a national border. Rumors abound that the UNHCR opposed the camp because the land was owned by Nicaraguans and that buying the camp would amount to giving land to the *contras*. The UNHCR also opposed another site favored by the Costa Rican government near Limón on grounds that it was not suitable for agriculture. Meanwhile, the UNHCR acquired land near Tilarán to expand the refugee camp there. The Costa Rican government objected on grounds that the nearby hydroelectric plant was a sensitive national security issue. Eventually a compromise was worked out whereby the additional land near Tilarán was used for agriculture but not for refugee settlements.

There are also difficulties in the actual administration of the camps. Until recently, IMAS administered the camps directly, but due to administrative difficulties (involving time-consuming bureaucratic procedures) this participation was being questioned by the government and alternative agencies were being considered.

There have been instances too where individuals have claimed refugee status in spite of their clear role in one of the armed forces active in the country. Given the activities not only of ARDE forces but of factions within the anti-Sandinista military forces, it becomes difficult to maintain refugee status as a strictly humanitarian category.

COSTA RICA AND MEXICO COMPARED

The Costa Rican government thus finds itself in a precarious position. Its long traditions of neutrality in foreign policy, of generous asylum policies, and of support for international agreements compel it in one direction while its economic and political problems seem to require a policy of limiting refugee admissions. While there have been some hints that Costa Rica might withdraw or attach reservations to its adherence to the UN protocol, so far, the government has not given in to these pressures. In spite of some governmental suspicion, the Monge administration has managed to extend legal recognition to many (though not most) Central American refugees and to provide some basic services to them. Yet the levels of Costa Rican economic ability and political tolerance have limits. The continued heavy flow of Central Americans could well test those limits.

The Costa Rican case offers an interesting comparison with Mexico. As in the case of Mexico, the Salvadoran refugees who have arrived in Costa Rica have tended to be concentrated in the cities while the refugees from the neighboring countries (Guatemalans in the case of Mexico, Nicaraguans in Costa Rica) have settled in the countryside. Both Costa Rica and Mexico have cooperated with the UNHCR in establishing camps or reception centers for the refugees coming from neighboring countries. In both countries, however, large numbers of refugees live among the local population without formal refugee status. In both cases, the range of estimates of the number of refugees is very wide, reflecting the difficulty of counting individuals who have been "absorbed" into the local population. Both governments have had difficulties with the UNHCR although those difficulties appear to have been more severe in the case of Costa Rica.

In both countries, a political culture exists that gives strong support to the ideal of generous admissions policies to politically-motivated migrants. Both countries see themselves as different from other Latin American nations in their tolerance of political diversity and willingness to accept dissidents from other countries. While both countries take pride in their revolutions, the Costa Rican revolution was much more limited in its impact than its Mexican counterpart. And yet governments of both countries use the rhetoric of their revolutionary experiences to justify both their foreign policy goals and their policies toward refugees. Costa Rica's foreign policy of stated neutrality and rejection of military force and Mexico's foreign policies of stated support for nonintervention and progressive governments can both be traced back to their historical experiences during the revolutionary period.

Both countries have always faced the necessity of developing foreign policies in response to their dependence on the United States. While Mexico has experienced much more direct intervention by the United States in its domestic affairs than Costa Rica, Costa Rica's smaller size and lesser strategic value have made it particularly weak in dealing bilaterally with the United States. In both cases, crushing foreign debts and economic crises have made the governments more sensitive to U.S. concerns. However, Mexico's greater economic leverage (both because of and in spite of, the debt) have made it less vulnerable to U.S. pressure.

The two governments differ in their foreign policies toward Central America. While both governments initially supported the Sandinista regime in Nicaragua, Costa Rican support has turned into overt opposition. This may be due in part to Costa Rica's feelings of vulnerability as a neighboring country. Interestingly, Mexico's greatest ambivalence in supporting progressive regimes also comes into play in relations vis à vis its neighboring country, in this case Guatemala. Relations with neighboring countries may also be especially tense because of national security concerns and the consequent greater participation of security forces in foreign policy decision making. Security forces—whether the Mexican military or the Costa Rican Rural Guard—are never known for their sympathy with revolutionary forces.

In both Mexico and Costa Rica, the existence of large numbers of refugees have complicated relations with neighboring governments. In both cases, the refugees' stories of brutality at the hands of government forces have fed popular opposition to the neighboring government. While both Mexico and Costa Rica are sympathetic to the plight of the refugees from neighboring countries, their dismal economic situations have served to prevent more generous policies of assistance (and in the case of Mexico, legalized status) to the refugees.

Costa Rica and Mexico differ with respect to their foreign policies toward El Salvador, although those differences may be narrowing. While Costa Rica has supported the present Salvadoran government and was quite enthusiastic about the 1984 Salvadoran elections, Mexico has been lukewarm, at best, with respect to the government and has sought to use its position to pressure for including the revolutionary forces in negotiations with the government. Similarly, Costa Rica has offered to use its good offices to facilitate negotiations between the government and the revolutionary forces while eschewing a more active mediatory role. As Mexico seems to be downplaying its support for the Salvadoran revolutionaries, the Costa Rican government seems anxious to preserve the appearance of independent action vis à vis the United States.

Both Costa Rica and Mexico have seen the issue of violence in Central America as a regional issue best resolved in regional forums. They have both condemned U.S. military actions in threatening Nicaragua, and both voted in the United Nations to deplore the U.S. invasion of Grenada. While Mexico has put most of its diplomatic efforts into the Contadora process, Costa Rica has been much more ambivalent in its response to the Contadora group. Although a Contadora team came to the Costa Rican-Nicaraguan border on a fact-finding tour in May 1983 (and found that the border was almost impossible to control), border incidents between Nicaragua and Costa Rica have continued. The Costa Rican government fears what it sees as a pro-Nicaraguan bias among some members of Contadora as well as other international fora such as the United States.

Another significant difference between the Mexican and Costa Rican responses to the Central American refugees concerns the existence of large numbers of armed exiles operating out of Costa Rican territory. The *contras'* activities have not been controlled by the Costa Rican government and are clearly a principal cause of the mass refugee flows out of Nicaragua into Costa Rica. The military actions by the *contras* have terrorized large segments of the rural areas of southeastern Nicaragua, leading to the flight of fearful Nicaraguan peasants, economic decline, and the increased militarization by the Nicaraguan government, including growing pressure on conscription of Nicaraguan youth. The continued operation of the *contras,* albeit with varying degrees of effort by the Costa Rican authorities to curtail their activities, indicates either official Costa Rican support for the *contras* (which given Costa Rican antagonism toward Nicaragua is not hard to imagine) or Costa Rican impotence in controlling its border and hence its national integrity. In either case, the continued operation of the *contras*—in spite of official Costa Rican neutrality—seems likely to continue. And of course, the more destruction wreaked by the *contras,* the more refugees who will flee Nicaragua, the more conflict between Nicaragua and Costa Rica, and indirectly the more U.S. pressure on Costa Rica to militarize in response to Nicaraguan "aggression" and military buildup. These armed exile groups—so-called "warrior communities"—further politicize the whole issue of Central American refugees. While the Guatemalan government has frequently charged the Mexican government with providing sanctuary to Guatemalan guerrillas in the refugee camps, these charges have been almost totally discounted by neutral observers. While undoubtedly some Guatemalan guerrillas hide in the Mexican jungle and launch attacks across the border, their numbers are very small in comparison with the Nicaraguan *contras* acting out of Costa Rica.

The existence of armed communities of exile groups is, of course, best known in the case of Honduras, where the existence of even larger *contra* forces have serious consequences for Honduran policies toward the Central American refugees. This study now turns to an examination of Honduran policies toward the Central American refugees.

5

Honduras: Caught in the Middle

Honduras borders on El Salvador, Guatemala, and Nicaragua, and individuals from all three countries are currently living as refugees within Honduran borders. The policies of the Honduran government toward the Central American refugees are both the most publicized and the most complex of any of the countries hosting large numbers of Central American refugees. The publicity stems from a longer involvement by Honduras than any other country in providing protection to the Central American refugees, particularly the Salvadorans. Furthermore, the involvement of many foreigners and many private voluntary organizations in the refugee camps has made the issue of treatment of the refugees a very political one. Controversies between the UNHCR and the Honduran government have been much more public because of the active participation of the nongovernmental organizations in those disputes. Moreover, Honduras has been the subject of intense pressure by the U.S. government to support its foreign policy interests in Central America, and—as a result—Honduran foreign policy has undergone significant changes in the past five years. In fact, Honduras is emerging as the government most likely to become more deeply involved in the conflict. Furthermore, as is the case with all the countries analyzed here, domestic economic difficulties coupled with an unstable political situation and growing popular political participation all make for a very complex and volatile political situation in Honduras. Honduran political traditions (and foreign policy objectives) also set it apart from the other countries presented here. The following sections detail the political culture, foreign policy objectives, current economic situation, and characteristics of the refugees currently seeking protection in Honduras.

A LEGACY OF POLITICAL INSTABILITY

Honduras has usually been considered as the least modern Central American country, and it has largely been free of the political violence that has characterized other Central American nations. Before 1950, Honduras clearly lagged behind the other nations in the region in terms of economic development. In 1957 President Ramon Villeda Morales declared that his was "the country of the '70s'—70 percent illiteracy, 70 percent rural population, 70 percent avoidable deaths."[1] While, like Costa Rica, Honduras was largely ignored by the Spanish crown, politics in the nineteenth century were dominated by both the liberal/conservative rivalry and the political instability so characteristic of Latin American politics. Indeed, from 1824 to 1950, the executive in Honduras changed hands over 116 times with only 13 leaders serving 4 or more years. But as J. A. Morris notes, "[i]n a sense, the 'bucolic' elite conducted political life with less volatility and harshness than in Guatemala or Nicaragua."[2] While politics were characterized by rapid executive turnover and exclusion of the masses from the political processes, the land tenure system that developed was quite different in Honduras than in the rest of Central America. Low population density and the dominance of foreign fruit companies as landowners meant that a local landed oligarchy did not develop in Honduras. With little pressure on the land, there was little motivation to destroy the older communal forms of landowning (the *ejidos*). The lack of a coffee oligarchy (due in part to the absence of a large landless workforce that could be used as migrant labor) meant less power to the Honduran landed elite. But the dominance of U.S. fruit companies was very important in Honduran development. The lack of pressure on the land meant that the fruit companies (principally United Fruit and Standard Fruit) had little incentive to use the land productively. Moreover, they were forced to import large numbers of black workers from the Caribbean (due to the fact that most Honduran peasants had access to land). They also acquired the country's best land. Yet S. Volk reports that as late as 1950, only 48 percent of the country's land was in private hands with the remaining 52 percent belonging to the state (31 percent) or to ejidos and other types of communal landholding. Within the private sector, however, there was great concentration of ownership in the hands of a few.[3]

The 1949 elections ushered in the beginning of important changes in the political system. In 1954, banana workers went on strike against the United Fruit Company. The 69 day banana strike resulted in victory for the workers and governmental recognition of the right to organize. Unfortunately, it was also followed by a massive reduction of the workforce on the plantations and the increased mechanization of banana production. Moreover, as Volk graphically explains, the successful strike led to a major shift in emphasis of the fruit companies away from direct production of fruit to greater reliance on control of marketing and commercialization of the product.[4] The election in 1957 of a reformist, Ramón Villeda Morales, led to moderate attempts at changing the political system. Villeda's efforts, however, were stifled by both the small middle class and by the United States (whose corporations controlled 95 percent of all foreign investment, including the country's infrastructure and vital exports). In 1961 Villeda pressed for agrarian reform. This move was very much in the spirit of the Kennedy administration's new Alliance for Progress, but also reflected the growing political clout and the increased militancy of the country's peasants. However, in spite of the spirit of the Alliance and the growing political muscle of the *campesinos,* United Fruit opposed the plan, jobs were lost, and Villeda was forced to cut back on the agrarian reform law. Villeda was somewhat more successful in passing laws in the area of labor and social security. Elections were scheduled for 1963, but when it looked like a Liberal Party candidate (who had made anti-military statements) might win, the army stepped in ten days before the election and installed Col. (later General) Oswaldo López Arellano, as president. López was to dominate the country's politics for the next decade.

The Honduran army had been involved in politics before, carrying out coups in both 1953 and 1957, and their professionalization occurred just as the civilian politicians were losing power. In times of civilian rule, the military had gradually reduced the power of the civilians; for example, the military had absolute power over military appointments and assignments. The military by the late 1960s had emerged as the most developed political institution in the country. Financially aided by the United States, the Honduran military attempted to establish order and stability. López rolled back the social legislation passed by Villeda and encouraged the industrial development of the country and especially foreign investment by U.S. corporations.

By the late 1960s—for the first time—Honduras faced real pressure on the land. The expansion of commercial crop production in the 1950s was a major cause of this pressure. As more land was used to produce export crops, the cost of staple foods rose as well. With the expansion of foreign investors on the land, the confiscation of peasant lands by Honduran agrarian elites, the lack of jobs in the cities, and the growing migration of Salvadoran peasants to the Honduran countryside, pressure mounted for a change. The distribution of wealth at this time was very unequal. About 60 percent of the labor force was dependent on agriculture while unemployment increased by 25 percent between 1961 and 1967.[5] The AIFLD (American Institute for Free Labor Development) tried to control the explosive situation but events escalated beyond their control. The labor unions in Honduras became the most politically aware and best organized in Central America.

In 1968 the government decided to impose higher sales and consumption taxes in a way that clearly benefitted the upper classes. The president used force to quell the resulting strikes and riots. As pressure on the government mounted, *campesino* activism increased. Finally, the Honduran government announced a new agrarian reform bill, which had the effect of forcing the Salvadorans to return home and which (as discussed in Chapter 2) precipitated a war with El Salvador.

The war further damaged the Honduran economy. While U.S. investment in Honduras skyrocketed,[6] Honduras was suffering serious balance of payments problems with the other members of the Common Market. The war in El Salvador offered a needed pretext for withdrawal from the CACM (the Central American Common Market).

Throughout the decade of the 1970s, the military and the Honduran landowners shared power in an occasionally uneasy alliance. As the U.S.-owned banana companies diversified into new areas and as unions developed into one of the strongest forces in Central America, López tried to coopt the opposition political leaders and to incorporate them into the government with token reforms. But the government was clearly corrupt. Revelations in 1975 showed that the Honduran government had cooperated with United Fruit in helping the company to realize substantial economic benefits. In 1975 a guerrilla peasant protest ended in the massacre of nine *campesino* leaders and ushered in what was for Honduras a new era in which violence was used for political purposes.

The military government of Paz García, which came to power in 1978, held peaceful elections for a constituent assembly in 1980. While the elections were relatively honest and had an 80 percent participation rate, the Army continued to rule the country until the presidential election in 1982. This resulted in the election of Roberto Suazo Cordova, the Liberal Party candidate, as president, but power still remained with the military, particularly with the commander in chief, Col. Gustavo Alvarez (known for his former position as head of the special police force, where he participated in repressive actions against leftists). In fact, it is reported that in a national television address in July 1982, "Alvarez expressed open admiration for Argentine methods of law and order and also declared open war on El Salvador's guerrillas."[7]

In the two years between the 1980 constituent assembly elections and the assumption of power by democratically-elected Suazo, the political situation in the country deteriorated. The discovery of clandestine cemeteries, the increasingly open activities of the death squads, and the growing actions of the leftwing guerrillas (including murder, hijackings, and bombings) all began to change the political climate of the country. Mass demonstrations with more than 60,000 people and the bombing of the Honduran Congress were manifestations of the country's growing polarization. The economic situation was becoming unbearable. The government's ever-closer collaboration with the United States and its perceptibly increasing involvement in the region's conflicts were the cause of great controversy. Discontent over the "orgy of corruption" among the military gave way to support for a change to civilian rule. But civilian rule, when it came, was to take place within the very narrow confines permitted by the military. As M. B. Rosenberg notes, "By late 1980, most high-level civilian politicians understood that the key to their success depended less on their ability to mobilize popular civilian support than in their relations with important Honduran military figures."[8]

If the key to Honduran politics was the role of the military, the key to the military was General Alvarez, who worked to ally himself with both the Liberal Party and with the U.S. government. Under President Suazo, the military has been allowed to control national security and foreign policy. But within the government and the military there were major behind-the-scenes struggles over how much Honduras should become involved in the Central American conflict. Suazo was limited by the military, and in fact a tacit agreement was reached prior to the elections that the civilian government would not look too closely into the military's past. Historically, COSUFA (Consejo Superior de las Fuerzas Armadas) was the chief decision-making body within the military, but Alvarez preferred to work independently and the power of that group was diminished.

There are many conflicts within the military. In 1980, Paz García dismissed 25 young liberal officers. Under the civilian regime, Alvarez' power was considerable. He was promoted to Brigadier General—a move that required special government action because it violated normal military procedures. Alvarez was very closely tied to U.S. foreign policy interests in the region. He was a close friend of U.S. Ambassador John Negroponte and repeatedly said "that all means are justified in the struggle against marxism."

Therefore it came as a surprise when on March 21, 1984, Alvarez resigned and fled to Costa Rica. The government announced that he had been discovered plotting against the air force and rumors abounded that he was planning to step up attacks against Nicaragua. There was also speculation that Alvarez was ousted because he was unwilling to cooperate with the Salvadoran military.[9] Air Force General López Reyes, who forced Alvarez to resign, became the new military chief of staff.

In mid-1984, the Honduran government seemed to be relaxing its clamp on dissidents, placing some restrictions on the freedom of the *contras* to move throughout the country, and putting some pressure on the United States to scale down the size of its military commitments. In August 1984 the cabinet was reshuffled to reflect these new priorities.

Under civilian rule, political parties in Honduras have become weaker. Suazo's Liberal Party has lost much of its vitality, due probably to the close ties between Suazo himself and the military. The National Party has turned away from its pro-military stance to criticizing military violations of the Constitution. As might be expected, given the continued importance of the military in the policy-making process despite the trappings of democracy, the Honduran Congress has lost power vis à vis the executive.

In November 1985 elections were held and the apparent winner was José Azcona Hoyo of the Liberal Party. The election was complicated by the existence of two different sets of electoral rules. While the constitution specifies that the individual receiving the largest number of votes is elected president, the supreme electoral law stipulated that the candidate of the party receiving the most votes would be president. In the Honduran case this meant that the candidate receiving the most votes, Rafael Callejas, was not elected president because Azcona's party received more votes (due to several candidates from the same party participating). The confused situation is likely to result in further confusion once the new government is installed. Moreover, Azcona will face a congress that is dominated by the opposition. Increasing reports of human rights violations in Honduras demonstrate the continued importance of the military in Honduran political life. Growing numbers of political prisoners and of disappearances have aroused fears of Honduran human rights organizations that the government will become more repressive.

Currently the military is divided between those who reject the military's participation in government and want to clean up corruption and those who oppose Suazo and view him as incapable of governing. There are elements within the latter group who favor not only military intervention but the establishment of a reformist military government (à la Peru) that would undertake basic socioeconomic reforms to prevent the further spread of revolution. The 1979 Sandinista revolution had a major impact on the military's view of their role in the country; it frightened them and led to a consideration of alternative strategies for preventing revolution. Thus there is now considerable emphasis being placed on civic action programs by the military.

The democratic opening of the late 1970s created new opportunities for Hondurans to organize, and mass organizations quickly formed. However, as the government has increasingly reflected the needs and wishes of the military and as domestic political violence has increased, there has been a real decline in the actions of the popular organizations. Leftist political parties and revolutionary organizations have grown weaker and more insulated. As conditions become more polarized, Rosenberg reports, the Church has become the most visible opponent of the regime.[10]

Honduran foreign policy, particularly with respect to El Salvador and the United States, has greatly influenced the conduct of its political culture. Honduran cooperation with the Salvadoran army has already brought the guerrilla struggle to Honduras and ever closer relations with the United States have provoked a popular wave of anti-American sentiment. While opposition to the government is mainly from moderate reformist groups, there is growing military pressure against the regime. The FPR (Popular Revolutionary Forces) and the MPL (Popular Liberation Movement) are the two principal Honduran guerrilla forces challenging the government.

Honduran political culture is thus characterized by the lack of legitimacy for political institutions, governmental instability, and by a feeling that Honduras is a weak, small nation that has been drawn into regional conflicts against its will. This political culture, unlike the cases of both Mexico and Costa Rica, has not been one stressing openness to political dissidents or a revolutionary democratic tradition. Rather, Honduras is still struggling to find its own identity and to work out its proper role in the Central American maelstrom. Into this turbulent, uncertain political system the Central American refugees have come, complicating the domestic process of conflict-resolution and resulting in a confused governmental response.

PRESSURES ON FOREIGN POLICY

As we have seen, Honduran policies within Central America have been marked by considerable hostility. Although the war with El Salvador was of very short duration and occurred over fifteen years ago, there is still widespread popular dislike of the Salvadoran military forces. Honduras' defeat in the 1969 war provoked a serious crisis within the Honduran military. Out of that humiliation came a strong desire to professionalize and to upgrade their military capabilities in order to ensure that such a defeat would never happen again.

Currently, Honduran military leaders view with great alarm the Nicaraguan military buildup. They feel threatened by the guerrillas' success in El Salvador and feel that their situation is unstable until the revolutionary momentum is overcome. This fear of revolution has led to a closer relationship between the Salvadoran and the Honduran military establishments. High military officials in Honduras and El Salvador have stated publicly that there will be no peace in Central America until the Sandinistas are removed from power.

The fear of a common enemy—revolution—has enabled Honduran military officers to cooperate with the Salvadoran military in at least certain areas.[11] Cooperation until 1980 was limited by the lack of a treaty between the two nations formally ending the 1969 war. In 1980, the Carter administration and the Salvadoran government alleged that the FMLN had established guerrilla bases in the demilitarized zones between Honduras and El Salvador. This area—three kilometers deep into each side—was nominally under the charge of the OAS, which was to ensure that neither army entered the zone. Quite suddenly in April 1980, shortly after the U.S. Congress approved its aid package to Honduras, there was a breakthrough in the hitherto stalemated negotiations. Honduras dropped its longstanding condition that the border line be finalized before relations could be improved. In November 1980 a peace treaty was signed that outlined a procedure for further border talks while restoring full diplomatic and economic relations.

This peace treaty paved the way for greater cooperation between the two armies. From the beginning this cooperation has been an uneasy one; the bitter memories of the war still linger. Indeed, as U.S. officials discovered in 1984 when they sought to construct a training facility for Salvadoran soldiers on Honduran territory, there was considerable resistance to the move among the Honduran military and political elite. And in fact, the United States was forced to change its plans. Honduras is reportedly still dissatisfied with the lack of progress in moving toward a final peace treaty with El Salvador.

For the U.S. government, Honduras plays a central role in its policies in the region. The United States seeks to foster cooperation between the military forces of Honduras, El Salvador, and Guatemala as a way of increasing their combined capabilities of withstanding revolutionary threats. U.S. pressure was largely responsible for the 1983 renewal of CONDECA, in which Honduras, Guatemala, and El Salvador agreed to act together as a "deterrent" to Nicaraguan aggression.

Honduras' geographic position has made it a key component of U.S. foreign policy in the region—a fact that both military and political forces are quick to exploit. Thus, during his July 1982 trip to Washington, President Suazo stated that Honduras "due to its geopolitical situation, is of fundamental strategic importance in pacifying the region and stabilizing democratic, economic, and social programs in Central America."[12] Suazo has been very supportive of U.S. interests in Central America and has been quoted as saying that all those who oppose the U.S. presence are communists.[13]

Historically, the United States used Honduras as a staging ground for its intervention into Guatemala in 1954 and has recognized the important role Honduras plays in the current situation in Central America. It appears that Washington's policy for Honduras is four-fold: 1) to use Honduras in support of the Salvadoran military's efforts to put down its revolutionary opponents; 2) to use Honduras as a staging ground for those *contra* forces trying to overthrow the Sandinista regime in Nicaragua; 3) to try to build up Honduras' military force as a way of preventing revolutionaries from directing their efforts at Honduras; and 4) to serve as a site for displaying U.S. force in the region.

Historically, the United States has been very important in the development of Honduran military forces. Between 1971 and 1980, the United States trained some 2,260 military personnel, and from 1976 to 1980, 100 Honduran officers attended the School of the Americans in Panama. As the violence in other Central American nations increased, Washington stepped up its aid to Honduras. In 1980 the United States extended $4 million in military aid and $45 million in economic aid, double the amount given in 1979. By 1984, the United States was giving $79 million in military aid and $39 million in economic aid. Since that time, projected aid for Honduras has gone even higher.

The U.S. military presence has not been limited to financial aid. Besides increased training of Honduran military personnel, approximately 300 U.S. military personnel are permanently stationed in Honduras—up from 24 in 1980, although under the Honduran Constitution, foreign troops can only use Honduras in transit.[14] As a result of U.S. aid and support, Honduran military capabilities have been dramatically enhanced. Honduras' 20,000 man army has become a powerful fighting force and its air force is the best equipped in the region. Runways have been built and rebuilt, new bases have been created, and the Honduran military is very proud of those changes. In fact, it may well be the case that the Honduran political establishment is manipulating the United States as much as the United States is using Honduras.

Originally, Honduras was important in Washington's plans for the region because of its geographic position as a possible conduit for arms from Nicaragua to El Salvador, and in November 1981 the Reagan administration approved $19 million in a CIA plan justified in terms of stopping the flow of arms from Nicaragua to El Salvador. As that argument began to disappear from official U.S. rhetoric (in part because the arms getting through were so few in number), the role of Honduras in supporting U.S. objectives also changed. Increasing aid and advisers were sent to Honduras to overthrow the Sandinista regime. Remarks by President Reagan in early 1985 indicate that the shift in stated U.S.

intentions is now complete and the United States is openly searching for ways to conduct war against Nicaragua. CIA advisers and arms from both the U.S. government and from private groups to the so-called *contras* have created a brutal war zone throughout southern Honduras. In spite of occasional efforts by the Honduran government to reduce the visibility of U.S. forces and to restrict the activities of the *contras*—who are extraordinarily disruptive of Honduran life—the U.S. efforts to overthrow the Sandinista regime from Honduran territory continue.

The U.S. government has been able to draw on Honduran fears of Nicaragua's military buildup and Honduras' military insecurity, in light of the revolutions sweeping the area, to draw Honduras ever more deeply into the conflict. Currently the Honduran/Nicaraguan border is the site of the most violence in Central America.

Behind the U.S. aid to Honduras has been a fear that if the revolutionaries in El Salvador were successful, Honduras would be threatened. Ironically, the U.S. presence may well turn out to be a self-fulfilling prophecy. U. S. military aid has increased the military power within the Honduran political scene and weakened civilian political institutions. As the government becomes less tolerant of dissent and as the death squads increase their operations, then the resort to armed revolutionary movements seems more likely.

It is in the area of displays of U.S. military force that Honduras has played the most visible role in U.S. policy in Central America. The United States has engaged in a series of military exercises designed to demonstrate both U.S. concern with Central America and superior U.S. military capabilities. Big Pine I in February 1983 was followed by Big Pine II from August 1983 to February 1984, involving some 4,000 U.S. and 6,000 Honduran troops, and by Ocean Venture in April 1984, which was the largest U.S. maritime exercise of all time, involving 30,000 U.S. troops at its peak. Honduras and the U.S. have agreed to continue joint exercises until 1988, although there are reports that such joint exercises are being planned for the next 25 years.

The construction of U.S. military facilities, including a large radar system, and the persistent reports of U.S. military involvement in actions launched from Honduran territory have created a substantial backlash among certain sectors of the Honduran population against the U.S. presence. There is a widespread feeling in Honduras that the country is losing control of its borders and becoming a lackey of the U.S. government.

This growth of popular anti-Americanism was accompanied by military discontent over increasing U.S. military influence, and this was manifested in April 1983 with the dispute over CREM (Regional Military Training Center). The U.S. proposed the establishment of a base in

Honduras (funded and staffed by the U.S. government) to train Salvadoran officers. Alvarez and Suazo agreed but the president of the Congress balked, pointing to the provision in the Honduran Constitution that no foreign military bases may be constructed on Honduran territory. Eventually, however, the Congress approved the plan in order to stop Nicaragua's "terrorist plans." A faction of the Liberal Party split off in opposition to CREM. There was substantial opposition within the military over the school and growing dissatisfaction with the nature of the Honduran-U.S. relationship. U.S. economic aid to Honduras was not as high as expected. In July 1984 Reyes asked the United States to change the ratio of 7 Salvadoran to 3 Honduran officers to one more beneficial to Honduran interests. And in September 1984 CREM stopped training Salvadoran military personnel.

As a consequence of this dissatisfaction at least some elements of the Honduran military began to talk of moving toward a noninterventionist policy.[15] Honduran foreign policies vis à vis the United States have produced a great deal of discontent in Honduras. There is a feeling that the United States runs the country and that Honduras is being dragged—against its will—into the Central American conflict. Thus the ouster of Alvarez reportedly came as a surprise to both U.S. Ambassador Negroponte (who was told about it beforehand) and to Honduran President Suazo (who was only informed after the fact).

In the past year, Honduran leaders have been showing greater independence vis à vis the United States. In September 1984 López reportedly closed two contra camps and one contra hospital and also reduced the size of future U.S. military exercises.[16] This opposition to the U.S. presence in the country—as well as to the deteriorating economic conditions—is manifest in increased political discontent. This, in turn, makes those in positions of power uncomfortable and leads to greater restriction of dissidents. Thus, in Honduras we see the steady deterioration of legitimate civilian rule and the destabilizing of another Central American country. The economic crisis facing Honduras—while not as severe in relative terms as those confronting Mexico and Costa Rica—is another destabilizing force.

DECLINING ECONOMIC CONDITIONS

Like the other Central American countries, Honduras has faced serious economic difficulties for the past decade. Honduras is above all, an agricultural country. Over 57 percent of its population works in the agricultural sector, most of which is geared to export to the U.S. market (coffee, bananas, meat, and timber). The growth of agricultural exports has led to an increase in food imports. Both Honduran agricultural exports and imports are dominated by U.S. corporations. Barry et al. report that the United States buys 60 percent of Honduran agricultural production and that in 1980 Honduras imported $51 million in food from the United States, up 61 percent from 1979.[17] Like other oil-importing nations, Honduras was badly hurt by the skyrocketing price of imported oil in the 1970s, which cost an ever-increasing quantity of Honduran agricultural exports.

Honduras' low rate of industrialization made it the principal loser in the Central American Common Market during the 1960s. The country was simply unable to compete with more efficient production from other member countries and complained bitterly about its maltreatment. Following the 1969 soccer war, the Common Market fell apart. However when efforts were made to re-establish the market, Honduras made sure that it would not suffer disproportionately (and also ensured the CACM's total demise) by imposing a 10 percent tax on products imported from the other member countries. The other members retaliated and the efforts to revitalize the common market were recognized as total failures.

As in the case of Mexico and Costa Rica, Honduras accumulated a sizable foreign debt and in 1981 imposed an emergency economic plan devised by the IMF as a necessary condition for receiving aid from that institution. The IMF-imposed plan called for decreasing imports, increasing exports, and measures to keep capital in the country (capital flight is estimated at $1 billion annually and increasing). Although the government fired 3,000 public employees and moved to implement some of the IMF measures, the situation deteriorated. Indeed Barry et al. estimate that by the early 1980s unemployment and underemployment reached 64 percent.[18] By 1983 the situation was even worse. The GDP fell by 0.7 percent in 1983 and the external public debt reached almost 37 percent of the GDP.[19] In August 1983 the debt was rescheduled but it failed to meet IMF standards. In March 1984, faced with a $300 million deficit, another austerity package was introduced that raised taxes and cut wages of government employees. The IMF still insists, however, on a devaluation of the currency before refinancing the debt.

Since 1980 the Honduran economy has been in a state of decline. Industry, traditionally never very strong, is currently operating at about 50 percent of capacity, 65 percent of the nation's firms have closed since 1982, and the construction sector is presently working at 10 percent of capacity. As in the other Latin American countries studied here, the human costs of the economic decline have been substantial. Almost 75 percent of all rural households presently live below the poverty level, while unemployment reaches 20 percent and underemployment another 60 percent. Currently there are 200,000 landless peasants in the country.[20] Moreover, Honduras has been greatly hurt by the continuing war along its border with Nicaragua. *Contra* and Sandinista activities have hurt livestock and made the land useless. Customers have been cut off from that region and there is virtually no trade. Moreover, the region's instability has scared off foreign investors. The Honduran military controls the budget, making it extraordinarily difficult for civilian political leaders who must take the political heat for budget decisions they ultimately cannot control.

In this climate of economic impotence, aid from the United States has been absolutely critical for the government. General Reyes has complained that while economic aid has fallen from $102 million in 1980 to $84 million in 1984, military aid has increased. What is needed, according to the general, is greater economic aid.[21] Thus Honduras is caught in a bind. It must have the goodwill of the United States in order to put its house in order, and the way to obtain that goodwill is by supporting U.S. foreign policy objectives in Central America and by adopting economic programs deemed essential to the International Monetary Fund. Honduras is, in fact, in a position of almost total dependence on outside forces. Clearly without a political culture that would justify a policy of neutrality or nonintervention, it would be difficult now for the Honduran government to make moves in that direction.

And so Honduras is drawn deeper and deeper into the Central American conflict. Its domestic political situation, in which the military is the dominant political force, its foreign policy of subservience to the United States, and its dismal economic situation have severely limited its autonomy. Furthermore, the fact that relatively strong unions still exist and that *campesino* unions are beginning to exercise real clout, together with the expectations generated by the accomplishment of democratic rule, have made it more difficult for Honduras to go quietly along with behind-the-scenes pressure applied by the United States. Into this complex situation, the Central American refugees have come—causing immense domestic and foreign policy dilemmas for the government.

THE CENTRAL AMERICAN REFUGEES IN HONDURAS

Three distinct exile groups are currently seeking protection within Honduran national borders. The largest group are the Salvadoran and Guatemalan peasants fleeing the repression of their rightwing governments. But there are also rightwing exiles from Nicaragua who are openly seeking to overthrow the Nicaraguan regime. Finally, there are the Miskitu Indians of Nicaragua, who have crossed the border in search of shelter with their ethnic kin, the Honduran Miskitus, as well as those who have joined the anti-Nicaraguan government forces of the *contras*. Each of these three groups poses a different problem to the Honduran government, and these problems are exacerbated by the fact that Honduras is becoming the central focus of the Central American conflict. The three groups of refugees place the Honduran government in a very difficult political and strategic position and create serious economic difficulties for this, the poorest of the region's nations.

The case of Honduras, like the case of Costa Rica, is also complicated by the fact that the armed warrior exile communities, the *contras,* are not by any criteria refugees at all. They are exiles, continuing the military struggle and choosing to launch military attacks against an existing government. Their presence in Honduras complicates the government's policies toward the "genuine" refugees and is used as a justification for toleration of other exile groups.

Refugees from El Salvador have crossed the border into Honduras since 1979. Virtually all were peasants driven out of their homes by military sweeps of the areas next to the border. Initially, few problems were reported with the refugees living in Honduras. In spite of lingering hostility from the 1969 war, the Honduran peasants welcomed the Salvadorans by sharing their meager resources. While the Honduran government did not recognize them as refugees, it allowed them to remain in the country even though it wanted them to stay as close to the border as possible. Since politically Honduras was not yet seriously involved in the Central American conflict, the refugees were treated in a humanitarian fashion. As the number of refugees increased, the Church and various nongovernmental organizations began to get involved in providing refugee relief.

By June 1980 there were 4,000 Salvadoran refugees in Honduras. By January 1981 there were approximately 18,000 and the Honduran government moved to regularize their status and move them into camps. By the end of 1981, that number had jumped to 25,000, 19,000 of whom were getting UNHCR assistance. According to the Lawyers Committee for International Human Rights, an additional 20,000 Salvadoran refugees live in Honduras outside the camps.[22]

The Guatemalan refugees came to Honduras later, with significant numbers only arriving in mid-1981. In August of that year some 1,800 Guatemalans crossed into Honduras and the government was forced to respond to their needs. Unlike the Salvadoran refugees, the Guatemalans who have sought protection in Honduras have been a largely "floating population" of refugees; their numbers correspond directly to the violence in Guatemala. When a particular military campaign is finished, the refugees drift back into Guatemala. Although the number of

Guatemalans in Honduras at any given moment is relatively small, those numbers can increase dramatically with very little warning.

HONDURAN POLICIES TOWARD THE REFUGEES

Formulation of Honduran policies toward the refugees has been complicated by the fact that Honduras is neither a signatory to the convention or the protocol on refugees, nor does it have a national agency charged with cooperating with the UNHCR. Although there are persistent reports that Honduras is actively considering ratification of the relevant UN convention on refugees, given the current difficult situation in that country such an action is probably unlikely in the near future. There is a fear in Honduras that ratifying the convention would force the government to give the same rights to refugees as to Honduran citizens. In the present economic climate—particularly with the high unemployment and underemployment rates—such actions would be impossible. However, both a 1976 national law on population and migration and the 1982 constitution recognize the right to asylum.

The Honduran government has allowed the UNHCR to play an active role in providing for the refugees, although since the Honduran government is not formally bound by the provisions of international treaties, the position of the UNHCR is essentially an ad hoc one. The normal procedure for UNHCR action is for a formal link to be set up between the UNHCR and the national authorities responsible for the protection of refugees. As J. Adelman explains, "The implications of this are twofold: (1) the UNHCR has no collegial affiliate to discharge its basic functions even though it has the support of international and foreign agencies, and (2) Honduran authorities are not bound by institutional stipulations on refugee "status" or "treatment." The first implication creates a higher degree of burden than is desired by the UNHCR. The second has profound ramifications on the ability of UNHCR to use the international legal infrastructure in support of its policies."[23] What this means is that the UNHCR operates in Honduras at the discretion of the Honduran government. In order not to jeopardize that frequently-precarious working relationship, the UNHCR in Honduras has been cautious about challenging governmental authority. As discussed below, constant security violations in the camps have placed the UNHCR in conflict with the Honduran authorities, although the UNHCR has chosen to handle the problems very quietly.

Since the very beginning of the refugee flows, Honduran policies toward the refugees have been shaped by its foreign policies. As discussed above, the gradual move toward cooperation with the Salvadoran armed forces played a very important role in shaping Honduran policies toward the refugees. On May 14, 1980, even before the signing of the peace treaty, the military forces of Honduras and El Salvador apparently cooperated in seeking to flush out guerrillas along the Rio Sumpul, which marks the border between the two countries. By most reports the military engagement was an all-out massacre. As thousands of Salvadoran peasants sought to cross the Sumpul River into Honduras in search of refuge they were pursued by the Salvadoran military, while simultaneously they were pushed back from the Honduran side by the Honduran military. An estimated 600 Salvadoran peasants were killed that day, including many women and children. Reports of the brutality were—even by Central American standards—incredibly violent.[24] In spite of denials by both the Salvadoran and Honduran governments that such a massacre had occurred, eyewitness reports continued to pour out of the two countries and the Honduran Bishops' Council denounced the massacre. Similar massacres with joint action by Salvadoran and Honduran military forces have been reported at the Rio Lempa in March 1981 and again at the Rio Sumpul in May 1982.

The signing of the peace treaty has meant that Salvadoran troops now operate in areas immediately adjacent to the border. Yet the refugees continued to stream into Honduras from the violence-stricken provinces of Cabanas and Chalatenango directly across the border. While initially the refugees were cared for directly by Caritas and other nongovernmental organizations (and the government did not recognize the refugee status of the arrivals), by January 1981 the Honduran government was forced to assume a more active role in providing for the refugees. On January 21, 1981, the Honduran government formed a National Refugee Commission (CONAPARE). On January 23 representatives of the different agencies working with Salvadoran refugees were called to a meeting where they were told that "for delicate reasons of security and control" the government wanted all Salvadoran refugees placed in camps controlled by a military commander.[25] Throughout 1981 problems persisted in dealing with the refugees. Relief agencies grew suspicious about rumored collaboration between the Honduran and the Salvadoran governments and stopped registering refugees with the government because they suspected the names were being turned over to rightwing death squads.

There were also problems in the administration of the camps. Since the Honduran government has not signed the UN protocols on refugees, the UNHCR has had to operate through the offices of the UN Development Program. Since November 1982 when the UNHCR and the Honduran government drew up a memo of understanding on the terms under which the UNHCR would operate in Honduras, the UNHCR office has been upgraded and enlarged. The office now ranks with Mexico City and San José as a regional sub-office, directly responsible to headquarters in Geneva. There are presently two UNHCR reception centers (at La Virtud and Guarita) and several roving protection officers. In an innovative arrangement, these UN officers are free to travel up and down the still-disputed border with El Salvador. In fact, no other government in the world permits such freedom of movement to international agencies.[26] However, on several occasions Honduran authorities have prevented UNHCR protection officers from going closer than three kilometers to the border. These restrictions are most likely to be imposed during joint military maneuvers—which is essentially problematical as they are precisely the times when refugees seek to cross the border. Relations between UNHCR and the Honduran government have been fragile. The Honduran government does not have the resources to provide for the refugees and hence is completely dependent on international aid for financial support. At the same time, the UNHCR is dependent on the goodwill of the Honduran government and thus is vulnerable to shifts in government policy.

In Honduras, an individual is not considered a refugee until he or she enters the camps and thus the UNHCR is powerless to intervene when refugees are harassed by Honduran authorities en route to the camps. Within the camps the UNHCR designated CEDEN (the Honduran Evangelic Committee for Development and National Emergency), which is funded by the World Council of Churches, to provide logistic oversight of the camps. Wheaton reports that CEDEN's selection over Caritas (a Catholic service agency with a long record of involvement in refugee issues) is indicative of the government's desire to control the refugees.[27] CEDEN divided responsibility for the camps, with Caritas responsible for La Virtud, World Vision for Guarita, and the Mennonites for Mapulaca (while the camp at Colomancagua had functional division of tasks).

Persistent complaints about the activities of one of the agencies, World Vision, complicated the provision of refugee relief. The complaints centered on collaboration between World Vision and the Honduran and Salvadoran security forces against the refugees. World Vision was also accused of pressuring the refugees to adopt fundamentalist religious beliefs as a precondition for food and medical services.[28] Although World Vision eventually left the camps, the difficulties of that agency reflected the complex and politicized nature of the question of providing for refugee relief.

Until the fall of 1981, many Salvadoran refugees lived across the border in Honduran villages and in a few camps near the border—

particularly La Virtud camp, which was only a few hundred meters from the border. But in the fall of 1981, persistent harassment of the refugee camps by Salvadoran armed forces led the government to move the refugees farther from the border areas. The attacks became so prevalent that many observers concede that they could not have occurred without the complicity and support of the Honduran government. The government officially decreed that henceforth refugees would be restricted to a zone not less than 30 kilometers nor more than 50 from the border. The area where the largest of the new camps, Mesa Grande, is situated is located on an arid plateau where it is extremely difficult for refugees to become self-sufficient. Arid, dry, and lacking basic infrastructure, 10,000 refugees live in Mesa Grande in isolation from the Honduran population. Many Salvadorans chose to return home rather than be transferred to Mesa Grande. Given the opposition of the refugees, there was considerable controversy surrounding the role of the UNHCR in participating in this move.

Internal problems within CEDEN made coordination between the agency and the UNHCR difficult. In January 1982 an internal power struggle within CEDEN led to the resignation of 50 of CEDEN's 150 workers including the Director. The leadership of CEDEN was replaced with a more conservative group; following intense negotiations the UNHCR finally assumed direct oversight of the camps. Speculation was rife that CEDEN had been marginalized from the camps for protesting the relocation of the refugees.[29]

Given the UNHCR's delicate position vis à vis the Honduran government, it was perhaps inevitable that considerable tension would develop between the voluntary agencies providing relief in the camps and the UNHCR officials. The agency workers were with the refugees on a daily basis and were acutely conscious of the constant security problems facing the refugees. When they reported these violations to the UNHCR officers, they were dismayed at what seemed to them to be the organization's indifference to their concerns.[30] But for the UNHCR, the task of balancing concerns over the safety of the refugees with the need to adopt conciliatory gestures toward the government in order to continue operations made the situation extremely sensitive. The 1981 relocation of the refugees brought these issues into sharp relief.

Since the relocation, the Honduran government has said that Salvadorans found outside the designated refugee zone would be subject to detention or expulsion to El Salvador. Although the move diminished the harassment of Salvadoran refugees in that particular camp along the border, military and paramilitary attacks by Salvadoran forces have persisted.

As the political situation in Honduras has become more heated and as Honduras has become increasingly drawn into the wars of its neighbors, it is not surprising that the refugees are the victims. Due in part to U.S. pressure and aid and also to the increasing predominance of rightwing military forces within the Honduran armed forces, there seems to be a consensus on the nature of the struggle between Honduran and Salvadoran military officers. In December 1981 Colonel Abraham Turcios, head of the Honduran National Refugee Commission, was asked about the relationship between the Honduran and Salvadoran militaries. He replied, "We have a common enemy—the guerrillas."[31]

With the presence of additional refugees from Guatemala, the situation of the refugees generally is becoming more difficult. El Tesoro is the only camp for Guatemalans in Honduras and Guatemalan refugees reportedly find their reception in Honduras to be "icy." Currently only about 500 Guatemalans are settled in El Tesoro. Many more Guatemalans are reportedly hiding across the border awaiting safe passage into Honduran territory. Since November 1982 the Guatemalan army has been harassing the camp through actions such as flights over the modest refugee homes and paramilitary forces visiting the camp.

The militarization of the region has clear negative consequences for the refugees. Since 1982 the UNHCR has reportedly been searching for alternative sites for the refugees away from the sensitive border areas. In their November 1982 memo of understanding the Honduran government agreed in principle to the relocation of the Salvadorans remaining near the border. While the UNHCR studied possible alternative sites for the camps, it was not until December 1983 that the Honduran government accepted a UNHCR proposal to re-settle the refugees farther from the border, in Olanchito in the department of Yoro. The UNHCR argued that such a move would enable refugees to become more independent, more secure, and to trade in local towns. However, some observers fear that dispersing the refugees will make them even more vulnerable to attack by Salvadoran forces. The fact that the proposed area for refugee relocation was only 60 miles from the new U.S. training base (for Salvadorans) at Puerto Castillo was seen as evidence of a governmental intention to further intimidate the refugees. There was also a fear that without the refugees' presence, the border area would become a staging area for U.S. or Honduran intervention in El Salvador.[32] The 20,000 refugees from the four affected camps—El Tesoro, San Antonio, Mesa Grande, and Colomoncagua—opposed the move. The UNHCR, meanwhile, insisted on the relocation, arguing that it was unable to guarantee the security of the refugees in their present location. Moreover, the UNHCR maintained that this relocation was in line with its general policy of moving refugees away from the border region. Workers in the agencies providing direct services to the refugees opposed the UNHCR insistence on relocation. They rejected the security argument given by UNHCR, seeing the move as part of a larger strategic plan of the Honduran government.[33]

On September 5, 1984, the Honduran government notified the UNHCR that it had rejected the proposed refugee relocation plan and said that it was necessary for the UNHCR to adopt repatriation measures. Three days later the Honduran Foreign Ministry sent a letter to the Salvadoran Foreign Ministry proposing a mass repatriation of Salvadorans. In December 1984 the Salvadoran government told the Honduran authorities that it was disposed to receive the refugees. Although the Honduran government has in the past repeatedly stated that it will not repatriate people against their will, there is considerable speculation that involuntary repatriation of the Salvadorans may be under consideration.

Relations between the refugees, the agencies, and the UNHCR continue to be tense. On August 29, 1985, Honduran soldiers entered the Colomoncagua camp, ostensibly searching for Salvadoran guerrillas. Ten refugees were taken prisoner by the soldiers, over the strenuous objections of the UNHCR and the agency workers present in the camp. Two refugees were killed, and a number of refugees were wounded. Immediately following the incident, Colonel Turcios announced that the refugees would shortly be relocated. UNHCR agreed with the relocation, provided it be carried out in a peaceful and humanitarian manner. The refugees protested the relocation order, charging that their security problems stemmed from the Honduran security forces and not from their proximity to the border. The agency representatives working in the camps generally supported the refugees, although they recognized the need to remain neutral in the controversy. With the international outcry over the military incursion into the camps and with the Honduran elections, the issue of the intended relocation gradually subsided. But serious protection problems remain for the refugees. Honduran military forces continually enter the camps and there have been numerous incidents of harassment, intimidation, and even killing of refugees. Given the Honduran government's belief that these refugees are subversives, it is likely that tension will continue to characterize their relationship with the government. Although the 1985 elections will probably bring changes in personnel responsible for refugees, Honduran antipathy toward the refugees will probably continue.

While it still seems unlikely that the Honduran government will repatriate the Salvadoran refugees, Honduran dissatisfaction with the present situation and especially with the protests of the refugees themselves and the agencies that work with them is evident. Honduran military chief Alvarez was quoted as saying "If you have guests in your house, you decide where they will sleep."[34]

The situation for the Guatemalan and Salvadoran refugees in Honduras is uncertain; ultimately their future is tied to what happens in their home countries. As M. Solberg graphically puts it, "Honduras is a snakepit in the midst of Central America. Refugees from three countries are crowded into camps whose presence in that country is at least as much a matter of international politics as it is a matter of safety from battles being fought in Guatemala, El Salvador, and Nicaragua."[35] The refugees complicate relations between Honduras and its neighbors. While the Honduran government says it will accept all refugees coming to Honduras from El Salvador,[36] the Salvadoran government does not see these migrants as refugees at all. In June 1981, the then minister of defense of El Salvador said

> at least 15 percent or 4,500 of the refugees along the border are considered to be subversives. . . . [among the real refugees] a large sector [exists] that appears to be refugees and are simply terrorists who go precisely to find refuge and then return, commit their misdeeds and go back.[37]

And in fact, there are members of the Honduran armed forces who see the refugees in the same way. Col. Elovi Sierra stated "[m]ost of these people [the refugees protesting the move] have relatives in the guerrilla forces. The government does not want our territory serving as a sanctuary for subversion."[38] Honduras is in a difficult political position regarding the refugees. As a poor country, it depends almost entirely on the UNHCR to provide basic relief to the refugees. Honduras simply does not have the resources to provide for the refugees. But the Honduran military and the civilian government clearly do not want to encourage more refugees from these countries. Given the historical animosity between El Salvador and Honduras, an increased inflow of Salvadoran refugees is simply not welcome. So, as L. Cohen says, "it would be bad propaganda for Honduras to shut down the reception center and kick out the United Nations. Instead, the military allows these structures to exist while seeking to subvert them every step of the way."[39]

Death, intimidation, and harassment have all become a way of life for some of the refugees—the Salvadoran and Guatemalan peasants—living in Honduras. For the other two groups of Nicaraguans—the *contras* and the Miskitus, the situation is quite different. While the Honduran government has limited the activities of Salvadoran and Guatemalan refugees, policies toward the *contras* and the Miskitus have been much less rigid. The creation of an army of Nicaraguan exiles (primarily former

National Guard soldiers) across the border in Honduras has become an issue of international concern. The *contras,* as they are called, have mounted numerous attacks across the border into northern Nicaragua, provoking fear among the local inhabitants of the border area, tension between the Honduran and Nicaraguan governments, and high Nicaraguan casualties. Amply supplied by the U.S. government, the Nicaraguan exiles have greatly increased the level of tension in the region and have triggered fears of a full-fledged international war in the region. The *contras* apparently enjoyed the full support not only of the former U.S. Ambassador, John Negroponte, but also of the Honduran government, which only recently sought to limit the activities or the mobility of the *contras*—unlike the case of the Salvadoran and Guatemalan refugees. The military purpose of the *contras* is unmistakable—the overthrow of the Sandinista regime—although the *contras* themselves are a varied lot including both those who tried to defend the Somoza government from the revolutionary forces as well as those who initially supported the Sandinista regime but subsequently became disillusioned with the actions of the socialist government.

It is important to note that the *contras* represent a group very different from the other types of Central American refugees. They are predominantly young men who have chosen to fight the Nicaraguan government from outside the country. In contrast, the Salvadoran and Guatemalan refugees in Honduras are overwhelmingly peasants who are fleeing the government-induced violence of their home communities. This latter group is not composed of willing participants in an armed struggle, but of the victims of a struggle not of their making. The question of how the families of the *contras* should be treated has raised thorny questions about the nature of refugee relief. The families (and by some accounts the supporters) of the *contras* have left Nicaragua and are currently living along the border in Honduras. The UNHCR has been reluctant to grant these individuals financial and humanitarian assistance as refugees because to do so would be interpreted as support for guerrilla movements. A number of nongovernmental organizations such as Friends of the Americas have tried to extend humanitarian aid to these individuals, but such aid is inevitably politicized. For example, when faced with the possibility that the U.S. Congress might not support continued funding of the *contra* forces, the Reagan administration simply announced that it would greatly increase its aid to the refugees in Honduras. These individuals are primarily *ladinos* (non-indigenous groups) and are culturally distinct from the indigenous groups of refugees currently in Honduras.[40]

The third group of refugees in Honduras—the Miskitus—have characteristics of both of the other two groups. As discussed above, the Miskitu Indian ethnic group transcends national borders; Miskitus live on both sides of the border although the Nicaraguan Miskitus have been more politically active. When the troubles began between the Miskitus and the Sandinista government, many Miskitus took refuge in Honduras. Some of these individuals joined the *contras* in taking up arms against the Nicaraguan government. Others simply sought an escape from the violence of their homelands. In January 1982, at the time of the forced displacement of Miskitus into government-designated camps, more Nicaraguan Miskitus fled across the Honduran border to seek refuge, raising the total there to some 14,000.

For Honduras, the problem of the Miskitus was the problem of dealing with another mass influx of destitute refugees. This time the 10,000 refugees inundated an area inhabited by only 20,000 Honduran Miskitus, creating a very high ratio of refugees to local inhabitants. The Miskitus were initially settled into a single large camp at Mocorón, but beginning in 1983 they have been moved into smaller agricultural settlements.[41] As in the other cases of refugee camps, the decision to disperse the single large camp into smaller settlements was resisted by the refugees. The administration of the camps has come under severe attack by those concerned with Honduras' growing military hostility toward Nicaragua and with the increased U.S. presence in Honduras.

The Miskitus in the small settlements enjoy freedom of movement and are allowed to work in the villages. Some Miskitus have settled south of Mocorón near the border and receive some assistance from private agencies, although the UNHCR refuses to assist them unless they relocate away from the border. During 1983 the UNHCR began assistance programs to 2,100 non-Miskitu Nicaraguans who did agree to be resettled in areas east of Tegucigalpa. An additional 3,000 Nicaraguans have settled in Danli, near the border, but the UNHCR refuses to assist them unless they move away from the border. Some of the Miskitus face serious security problems as Misura, the military organization of Steadman Fagoth, has appointed local coordinators in the scattered Miskitu settlements to recruit (forcibly if necessary) men into the anti-Sandinista forces and to take charge of distribution of relief supplies provided by international agencies. The presence of a UNHCR protection officer in Mocorón has had only a limited effect on the problem, and in November 1983 U.S. evangelical groups providing relief to the Miskitus threatened to suspend their aid unless Misura coordinators were dismissed and forced recruitment stopped.

Honduras thus continues to be at the center of the refugee controversy, giving sanctuary with varying degrees of welcome to the victims of the violence in El Salvador and Guatemala, to the Nicaraguan exiles leading the military campaign against the Sandinista government, and to the Nicaraguan Indians searching for indigenous autonomy through links with the *contras*. Decisions on the refugees—how to treat them, what legal protections to extend, and so on—will depend on the political/ military conduct of the revolution in Honduras' neighboring countries.

Like both Costa Rica and Mexico, Honduras finds itself increasingly being pulled into the Central American conflicts. Unlike those two countries, however, the lack of a tradition of an independent foreign policy limits the government's ability to maintain some distance from the conflict. Without a tradition of either a defiant foreign policy (as in Mexico) or of neutrality (as in Costa Rica), Honduras has no indigenous tradition that it can draw on to resist being drawn in on the side of the United States. While, as we have seen, both Mexico's independent foreign policy and Costa Rica's neutrality have been seriously compromised by the reality of responding to contradictory pressures, nonetheless those independent traditions give the governments a source of national support for pursuing policies at odds with the United States.

All three of these Latin American countries are besieged with economic problems, and governments of all three fear that the revolutionary movements in Nicaragua, El Salvador, and Guatemala might take advantage of the discontent stemming from these economic pressures to foment rebellion there. All three of the governments—in spite of differences in rhetoric—would like to see stable democratic regimes in these three violence-racked countries. Democratic governments in those countries are perceived as legitimizing the current regimes of all three governments hosting refugees. All three of the governments resent the presence of the refugees as they complicate foreign relations with neighboring countries and pose additional economic burdens at a time when all of the governments are under serious pressure.

Unlike the Costa Rican and Mexican governments, Honduran actions toward the refugees are largely consistent with its foreign policy goals. The reception of refugees from friendly, ideologically similar governments (El Salvador and Guatemala) has been cool while refugees from an opposing government (Nicaragua) have been treated well. The government is limited in its policies by the fact that there is considerable popular support for revolutionary movements in the region. The government cannot afford to risk alienating large segments of its own population by treating the Guatemalan and Salvadoran peasants harshly or by openly expelling them. The government is also limited by its lack of economic resources. Honduras is dependent on international agencies to provide for the refugees, a fact that gives these agencies considerably more power than in a nation, such as Mexico, which is less needy of international assistance.

While the refugee situation in Honduras is the most complex of the three countries examined thus far, the absolute scale of the refugee problem is perhaps greatest in the United States, where the pressures to develop refugee policies in accord with foreign policies are in sharp relief.

6

The United States: The Politics of Exclusion

A constant theme throughout this study has been the central role of the U.S. government, both in affecting the conditions that have displaced some two million Central Americans and in influencing the policies of the host governments. While the causes of the political violence in El Salvador and Guatemala are largely indigenous, the internationalization of the conflict by the United States (and to a much lesser extent by Cuba) has contributed to higher civilian casualties. Massive U.S. aid to the Salvadoran government and the failure to use this aid to secure improvements in human rights has undoubtedly been a factor in displacing massive numbers of Salvadorans. Aid to the *contras* has similarly created a climate of terror along Nicaragua's borders. What had been low-level border skirmishes by remnants of Somoza's National Guard have become a force of well-armed men perhaps larger in number than the Honduran military. The continued violence has led many Central Americans to leave their homes and prevented those living in exile from returning home. Not only is the U.S. role crucial for understanding the root causes of Central American refugee migrations, but the U.S. government has played an important role in influencing the policies of other governments hosting large numbers of refugees. Mexico, Costa Rica, and Honduras have all been influenced by U.S. policies in developing their own refugee policies.

U.S. foreign policy objectives are thus central to understanding patterns of regional response to Central American refugees. U.S. policy toward those Central Americans seeking entry into the United States is formulated within a political culture emphasizing the nation's immigrant roots and foreign policy objectives of opposition to revolutionary change in the region. While the U.S. immigrant tradition has always existed more in theory than in fact, in recent years public opinion has become more supportive of restrictive immigration policy. Most obviously, U.S. policies toward the Central American refugees reflect the Reagan administration's foreign policy objective of stopping the spread of revolution in Central America. Given this objective, it is necessary for the U.S. government to restrict immigration of Central Americans who come from friendly regimes and claim political persecution; it would be inconsistent for the U.S. to do otherwise. And since El Salvador and, to a lesser extent, Guatemala are given political, economic, and military support by the U.S. government, to admit Guatemalans and Salvadorans claiming political persecution at the hands of their governments would prove embarrassing to U.S. policymakers.

The sections that follow outline the determinants of U.S. refugee policy in terms of national political culture, foreign policy objectives, and economic conditions. The nature of the refugee migrations and U.S. policies toward the refugees are then presented.

THE DOMESTIC CONTEXT OF U.S. IMMIGRATION AND REFUGEE POLICY

As a "nation of immigrants," the United States has always been particularly sensitive to immigration issues. U.S. political culture has stressed the nation's traditional welcome to the persecuted and downtrodden of the world. But, as Keely points out, U.S. concern with those seeking a new life has not been consistent over time:

> The United States has always been of two minds about new immigrants. On the one hand, the country has historically been a refuge, a place of new beginnings, accepting and even recruiting new settlers to build the nation and its economy. On the other hand, the theme of protectionism has found recurrent expression in apprehension over the capacity of the culture and economy to absorb newcomers, in the desire to limit labor market competition and assure minimal health standards and even in nativism and racist theories. The history of immigration policy is a dialectic of these two themes of acceptance and protection.[1]

The era of unrestricted immigration began to end in the late 1800s when provisions to exclude the sick, the criminal, and those with "unacceptable morals or political beliefs" were implemented. This was followed by the national origins quota acts of the 1920s, although Congress hesitated to halt immigration from the Western hemisphere because of a traditional U.S. foreign policy of Pan-Americanism and because of regional economic concerns. Indeed, during the 1920s, 1.5 million people emigrated to the United States from the Western hemisphere.[2] Thousands of these immigrants were people displaced by the violence of the Mexican revolution and at least one observer has seen in them the prototype of the Central American refugee flows of the 1980s.[3] By and large, however, the U.S. government did not distinguish between refugees and other types of immigrants until a much later period.

U.S. openness to the victims of political persecution has never been as great as popularly believed. During World War II, few victims of Nazi repression were admitted to the United States and in fact even the fairly large German quota went unused. However in 1948 the Displaced Persons Act provided for the resettlement of almost 380,000 refugees from the European wars.

U.S. refugee policy has been predicated on the assumption that the United States was a country for permanent resettlement and not merely a temporary haven from which people could be repatriated after stability in their homeland was restored.[4] While U.S. immigration law generally responded to the U.S. need for labor (with a few minor exceptions), political refugees have had to gain admission to the United States within the same framework as other immigrants.[5] Thus, at those times when U.S. economic needs for labor were low, admission of individuals fleeing political persecution was limited.

The 1965 Immigration Act eliminated discrimination against Asians, mandated an end to the national origins quota system, and placed a ceiling on visas for immigration from the Western hemisphere. Refugee status was limited to those fleeing Communist-dominated countries or the Middle East and limited to 6 percent of total visas. Western hemisphere residents were automatically excluded from eligibility and fairly rigorous criteria were required for admission (for example, the individual had to show that flight had been necessary, that persecution came from governmental or quasi-governmental sources, and that he or she had not been firmly resettled between the time of leaving and applying for asylum). However provision was made in the immigration law, under the parole power, for the Attorney General to allow entry for up to two years of any person whose admission was deemed to be in the national interest. This was envisaged as an emergency measure but was frequently invoked at the urging of members of Congress for Hungarians, Indochinese, Cubans, and other groups.[6] The changes embodied in the 1965 Immigration Law reflected the nation's healthy economy as well as the growing tolerance and political power of ethnic groups.

The use of the Attorney General's parole authority created a system in which refugees were first screened abroad and then admitted in accord with their rank order on waiting lists. Nearly two million aliens entered the U.S. in this manner to the positive political benefit of the U.S. government. The numbers and activities of entrants could be strictly controlled and a domestic backlash could be avoided. This made it possible, as Scanlan and Loescher point out, to maintain, without much difficulty, a refugee admissions system almost entirely independent of U.S. immigration law, under the direct control of the executive (rather than the legislative) branch and dedicated to a few consistent, but limited, policy ends.[7]

Thus U.S. refugee policy before 1980 was explicitly designed to reflect foreign policy objectives. By defining refugees solely as products of communist governments or Middle Eastern states, the U.S. government ensured that its refugee admissions policies would directly support foreign policies based on a Cold War mentality. Policy toward refugees was firmly in the hands of the executive; although Congress sought to influence the process on behalf of certain groups, it was the executive branch that decided whom to admit. The United States accepted almost half a million Vietnamese refugees between 1975 and 1980, reflecting U.S. concerns with Indochina and the "destabilizing effect of large refugee populations in a part of the world deemed vital for national security."[8]

On March 17, 1980, Congress passed the Refugee Act of 1980 with the objectives of providing a "permanent and systematic procedure for the admission of refugees of special humanitarian concern to the United States" together with "comprehensive and uniform provisions for [their] effective resettlement and absorption."[9] Refugees were defined in U.S. law in accord with the convention of 1951 as those individuals outside their homelands who are unable or unwilling to return because of persecution or a well-founded fear of persecution. This act eliminated the statutory preference for victims of communist governments and constructed an elaborate bureaucratic structure for processing and dealing with the refugees. The parole authority of the 1965 Immigration Act was replaced with new statutory language asserting congressional control over the entire process of admitting refugees. The annual limit on regular refugee admissions was raised from 17,400 to 50,000 and the Act provided that that number could be raised after annual consultations with the Congress. The Act also provided for an explicit asylum provision in the immigration law that included a lengthy appeals process. The assumption, of course, was that very few asylum cases would be filed.

As A. H. Leibowitz notes, the 1980 Refugee Act, by changing the definition of refugee, created serious problems for future admissions policies. While the number of refugees who would be eligible for refugee status in the United States was increased from about 3 million to 13 million (by eliminating the geographic restrictions), the United States established clear numerical limits on responding to those refugees. "Congress had, consciously or unconsciously, created large numbers of claimants who could not be satisfied."[10] It became particularly difficult to deal with refugees from generalized political oppression.

Under the Refugee Act a full range of federal programs was created to assist in the resettlement process. The Office of the U.S. Coordinator for Refugee Affairs and the Office of Refugee Resettlement (within the Department of Health and Human Services) were created. But the creation of these institutional mechanisms was based on the assumption that refugees would be processed abroad, that determination of refugee status would take place in regions geographically removed from the United States, and that only then would the refugees be transported and resettled in the United States. In fact, this had been the situation with the 1979 mass migration of Indochinese refugees. In spite of the problems caused by their tremendous numbers, U.S. refugee policies could be developed and largely implemented in Indochina. The 1980 Refugee Act reflected both executive and congressional concerns with the Indochinese refugees and was based on the assumption that future refugee situations would be similar in nature (though hopefully not in scope) to the Indochinese experience.

While the Refugee Act of 1980 created a complex set of agencies and procedures designed to regularize the flow of refugees, it was immediately challenged by the Cuban Mariel boatlift of April 1980 in which 150,000 Cubans migrated to the United States in a mass exodus that overwhelmed the procedures established in the Refugee Act. The Cubans came to the United States as their country of first asylum, immediately calling into question the assumptions on which the Refugee Act was based. Instead of being resettled in the U.S. in accord with determinations made by U.S. officials in the field, the Cubans arrived directly in Florida creating an administrative nightmare for those involved in determining their status. Furthermore, the Cubans were using the procedures for political asylum instead of the carefully crafted mechanisms for refugees. The asylum procedures (spelled out in more detail below) required the Immigration and Naturalization Service (INS) to make a determination of political persecution on an individual basis, based on investigations into the individual applicant's background and on State Department opinions of the case. The new bureaucracies created by the Act were overwhelmed. INS lacked the personnel to interview every person seeking asylum and the State Department lacked the personnel to research the advisory opinions required in asylum cases.

President Carter stepped in and re-asserted his parole authority to respond to the mass migration. When controversies ensued over the perceived preferential treatment of Cubans (in comparison with the waves of Haitians who had been detained and deported), President Carter bypassed the refugee system completely, creating a new category, Cuban/Haitian entrant, as a temporary status. Not only did this decision reveal the inadequacies of the new legislation, but it may have also contributed to the backlash against the Cuban entrants by forcing local communities to pay the resettlement costs. The experience of the Cuban refugees raised serious questions about the utility of the 1980 Refugee Act, particularly in cases in which the United States is the first country of asylum. The politicization of U.S. refugee policy was further underscored in February 1984 when the Reagan administration announced that it was moving to regularize the "temporary" status of the Cuban entrants, but was not extending similar treatment to the Haitians (who were given the same status as temporary entrants in 1980 along with the Cubans).[11]

Latin American immigration issues are particularly sensitive in the United States, given the traditional problems caused by illegal immigration of Mexicans to the United States, the growing social and political presence of Hispanics among the U.S. population, and the politicization of immigration questions in light of high unemployment in the U.S. Southwest. But for the most part, the U.S. has very little experience with politically-motivated migrations. In spite of the relatively large flows of Latin American political exiles out of the region over the past decade, most went elsewhere and very few were admitted to the United States. All told, Latin America plays a minor role in official U.S. refugee policy. For fiscal year 1983, the U.S. government approved a refugee ceiling of 90,000 including only 2,000 for Latin America. In 1984, that ceiling was reduced to only 1,000. In fact, as discussed below, even fewer Latin Americans are actually granted refugee status.

In spite of the long tradition of Latin American migration to the United States and despite the elaborate procedures spelled out in the 1980 Refugee Act, the overwhelming majority of those Central Americans arriving in the United States are not treated as refugees and are not granted the benefits accruing under U.S. law. The Central American refugees come to the United States illegally and typically come to the attention of the State Department and INS authorities only after being apprehended for illegal entry. Thus, they tend to use the asylum mechanism rather than the refugee process in seeking protection from the violence of their homelands. Given the context of U.S. immigration and refugee policy, the illegal nature of the Central American refugee flows makes it very difficult for policymakers to develop and apply consistent policies. Moreover, as discussed below, the foreign policy interests of the U.S. government are a principal determinant of U.S. policies toward the region.

U.S. FOREIGN POLICY OBJECTIVES

From U.S. adventurer William Walker's forays into Nicaragua in the mid-nineteenth century to the CIA-backed invasion of Guatemala in the mid-twentieth century, the U.S. government has been intimately involved in Central American politics since those nations became independent in the early 1800s. Current U.S. foreign policies are shaped by and interpreted within the context of this interventionist legacy. While contemporary analysts differ in their assessment of the relative importance of economic versus strategic interests for the United States, all agree that U.S. policies toward Central America play a central role in the region's political development. Although a comprehensive discussion of U.S. policies in Central America is beyond the scope of this work (and has been done elsewhere), several themes are apparent.[12] U.S. policy toward Central America occurs within a historically "close" relationship. As with all of Latin America in general, U.S. rhetoric of a "special relationship" with Central America and the development of inter-American institutions structures and shapes relations between the U.S. and the region.

Currently, the United States has substantial economic and strategic interests in Central America. As Table 6.1 shows, U.S. investment has increased dramatically over the years; currently 70 of the 100 largest U.S. corporations do business in Central America. While most U.S. direct investment is located in Panama, due to the presence of the International Financial Center, the Colon Free-Trade Zone, and an infrastructure providing energy and transportation, there is considerable corporate investment throughout the region. In 1979, the Department of Commerce reported that the rate of return on U.S. direct investment in Latin America was 19.6 percent while the average international rate of return for U.S. direct investment was only 7.6 percent. Not only is Central America important to U.S. corporations for direct investment, but the region also provides an annual market for $2.6 billion in sales of U.S. goods. The United States provides 56 percent of the manufactured products imported into Central America. Moreover in recent years private banks have become heavily involved in Central America. In 1980, total Central American external debt stood at $10.7 billion, almost half of which came from the private sector.[13]

Yet considering the context of total U.S. corporate investment and financial interests abroad, Central America occupies a very minor role for U.S. corporate interests. The Central American debts, while overwhelming to Central American governments, represent a very small proportion of outstanding debts in the Third World. Mexico and Brazil, for example, each owe more than ten times the amount owed to foreign financial interests by all the countries in the Central American region. Economically, the state of U.S. business and financial health is much more dependent on the larger Latin American and other Third World countries than on what happens in Central America. Similarly, the United States does not depend on Central America for imports of strategic materials. While particular corporations—especially fruit, timber, and cattle corporations—are deeply involved in Central America, overall the level of U.S. economic interests in the region is limited.

Table 6.1: U.S. Direct Investment in Central America by Country, 1977 and 1980 (millions U.S. $)

	1977	1980	Percent Change
Belize	21	24	15
Costa Rica	178	303	70
El Salvador	79	103	30
Guatemala	155	226	46
Honduras	157	288	83
Nicaragua	108	89	18
Panama	2,442	3,190	31
Central America	3,140	4,223	34

Sources: Tom Barry, Beth Wood, and Deb Preusch, *Dollars and Dictators: A Guide to Central America* (Albuquerque: The Resource Center, 1983), 40.

However, while economic interests are limited, U.S. strategic interests in Central America have acquired increased importance. The Nicaraguan insurrection caught the Carter administration by surprise. Although the United States adopted a variety of tactics toward the revolution during the course of the insurrection, one of the participants in these U.S. policies summarized that period by noting that "the U.S. [had] worked hard to prevent the Sandinistas from acceding to power."[14] However, when faced with the fait accompli of a successful insurrection, the Carter administration adopted a cautious policy of tolerating radical rhetoric and seeking to moderate the course of the revolution. During the year following the Sandinista victory, the U.S. government extended substantial financial aid to the regime. But the process of approving the aid was so drawn-out and, for Nicaragua, so humiliating that the aid was not seen as a gesture of goodwill but rather as an attempt to influence the revolution's outcome.

While the Carter administration had reacted cautiously to developments in Central America, giving modest support to the FSLN and encouraging less repressive policies in El Salvador, the Reagan administration saw the conflict in different terms. Central American revolutions were viewed not as the products of indigenous situations of inequality and domestic revolutionary movements, but rather as financed and directed from abroad by communist powers seeking to extend their penetration into a U.S. sphere of influence. During the 1980 campaign, Ronald Reagan pointed to Nicaragua—as well as to Afghanistan and Iran—as evidence of both Carter's softness on communism and the declining U.S. power in the world. Given this worldview, the Reagan administration launched an offensive against the revolutionaries in Central America. On February 27, 1981, Secretary of State Haig indicated the need for punitive actions against Cuba when he stated "Cuban activity has reached a peak that is no longer acceptable in this hemisphere . . . El Salvador is a problem emanating first and foremost from Cuba . . . it is our intention to deal with this matter at its source."[15] In March 1981 the Reagan administration authorized funding for the *contras* and cut off remaining economic assistance to Nicaragua. As Smith explains, "[T]his was a colossal blunder. Not only was the United States thus identified with the Somocistas and a 'return to the past,' but the fact that Managua was threatened by a Somocista/CIA operation subsequently made it difficult for more democratic opponents to raise the banner against the radical Sandinista commanders."[16]

Aid to the *contras* was justified in terms of interdiction of arms shipments from Nicaragua to El Salvador—to "stop the spread of communism in this hemisphere" and an elaborate white paper was produced to justify such aid. In El Salvador the Reagan administration increased its military and economic support for the Salvadoran government and sought to prevent a military victory by the guerrilla forces at the same time they tried to curtail the blatant violence of the Salvadoran rightwing and to present the regime as a moderate, struggling democracy. In Guatemala the Reagan administration downplayed the regime's brutality and began to renew its ties with the military regime. And, as has been noted, U.S. aid to Honduras was greatly expanded.

U.S. interests in Central America have been three-fold: 1) to witness the defeat of the Sandinista regime; 2) to prevent a communist victory in El Salvador; and 3) to strengthen stable, preferably moderate, democratic regimes committed to free enterprise. In his February 1985 news conference, Reagan's assertion that he intended to "make the Sandinistas cry uncle" made U.S. interests regarding the Sandinistas all too clear. By militarily supporting forces hostile to the Sandinistas—both within and outside the country—the Reagan administration has defied international law and national public opinion. The mining of Nicaraguan harbors and revelations of CIA-published assassination manuals were unpopular acts. In reviewing public opinion data on Central America, William LeoGrande concludes:

> By fairly wide margins, the public has disapproved of the way in which the president has handled the Central American crisis and has opposed almost every specific policy initiative set forth by the Administration, from economic and military aid to the deployment of U.S. military advisers and the launching of the covert war against Nicaragua.[17]

Nonetheless, military aid to Central America has dramatically increased under the Reagan administration. The administration introduced the Caribbean Basin Initiative as a way of encouraging Central American exports and the development of free enterprise in the region. Although initially very enthusiastic about prospects for industrial growth, Central American governments have come to see such efforts as far less than what is needed to change fundamentally the desperate economic situation in which they find themselves.

U.S. foreign policy toward Central America under the Reagan administration has been characterized by extreme and increasing hostility toward the Nicaraguan Sandinista regime, and by military and economic support for the Salvadoran government. In the latter case, an essential component of the administration's strategy has been to present the Salvadoran government as a moderate democratic alternative to Cuban-based revolutionaries. Thus the 1984 elections, boycotted by the left, were showcased by the administration as evidence of democracy at work. Although there has been some rhetorical support for the Contadora process, the U.S. government has made it clear that it prefers a bilateral approach to the region's conflicts. Such an approach increases the power of the U.S. government to exert leverage over a situation deemed vital to national security. In this context, the claims of Central American refugees seeking protection in the United States must be denied. Their presence—particularly their visible and legal presence—brings contradictions in U.S. policies into sharp focus.

ECONOMIC FACTORS

Economic factors have been relatively less important in determining U.S. policy toward Central American refugees than in the other major host countries. The much greater overall economic capacity of the United States combined with its relative stability and an existing infrastructure for processing and providing for refugees set the United States apart from all Third World countries. Even in times of high inflation and/or unemployment, few questioned the ability of the U.S. government to provide for the refugees in the short term.

The larger questions stemming from the North American economic system concern the distribution of limited resources in the future. The national debate over immigration reform and the ultimate composition of U.S. society has been influenced by a realization that the United States can no longer be a country of refuge for all oppressed peoples of the world. Distinctions between immigrants coming to the United States because of poverty and those fleeing political persecution are not generally made. W. A. Cornelius notes that the anti-immigration sentiment is partially the result of economic uncertainty. "Many of the people who are angry about the give-away programs for illegal aliens are also angry about the treatment which they themselves receive from the governmental system."[18] But popular opposition to immigration has roots deeper than immediate economic concerns; Americans feel that they have lost control of their borders and "seem to have a need *to believe* that immigrants are to blame for their own problems."[19] However, data on the relationship between economic conditions and public attitudes toward admission of refugees should be treated with caution. A 1984 survey commissioned by the U.S. Committee for Refugees showed that while there is an abstract opposition to admission of more immigrants, when individuals were asked about specific cases, they were very supportive of expanding refugee admissions. Moreover, the study found a relationship between lack of knowledge of refugee/immigration issues and opposition to refugee admissions. Since a vast majority (91 percent) of those surveyed describe themselves as either not well informed or having no opinions on refugee issues, this would seem to indicate the possibility for a radical change in public attitudes toward refugees.[20]

As in the other countries studied, the principal reason given for public opposition to increased refugee admissions is the pressure for jobs in an era of high unemployment. As in Costa Rica, the existence of a social welfare system to provide assistance to legal immigrants also raises fears about the governmental expense of providing basic services to the refugees. Historically, when the national economic situation declines, opposition to immigration generally and to refugee admissions in particular increases. In this context, the Central American refugees have raised new fears about the system's ability to provide for them.

THE CENTRAL AMERICAN REFUGEES IN THE UNITED STATES

The number of Central Americans arriving in the United States has steadily increased with the escalation of violence in the region. Indeed, an estimated 10 percent of El Salvador's five million people currently live in the United States, along with growing numbers of Guatemalans and Nicaraguans. Central Americans fleeing their war-ravaged lands have followed traditional routes of economic migration and are concentrated in U.S. cities with high Central American populations, such as Los Angeles, Washington, D.C., and New York. The Central Americans are overwhelmingly motivated by fear—fear of being singled out for persecution by the notorious death squads and fear of being caught in the crossfire of military encounters between the guerrilla forces and the government. But the Central American wars have taken a high economic toll as well: counterinsurgency campaigns have destroyed villages and crops, declining industrial production and capital flight have made imported goods scarce, and guerrilla attacks on infrastructure have damaged the national economy. Thus, while the Central Americans flee violence and political persecution, they also seek to escape the economic devastation of their countries. Estimates of the number of Salvadorans in the U.S. vary greatly, reflecting difficulties in estimating illegal entries, but estimates generally range between 300,000 and 500,000.[21] By early 1984 officials of various governmental and nongovernmental organizations privately estimated the number of Salvadoran refugees in the U.S. at around 750,000.[22]

The policies of the other governments hosting large numbers of refugees influence U.S. policymaking toward the refugees. The U.S. government argues, for example, that the Central Americans arriving at its borders should not be granted refugee status because they have chosen to leave their countries of first asylum—for example, Mexico —for the United States. While their decision to leave El Salvador, the reasoning goes, may have been for political reasons, they choose to come to the U.S. for essentially economic reasons. As Peter Larabee, Director of the INS Detention Facility at El Centro, California, stated, the Salvadoran refugees "are just peasants who are coming to the U.S. for a welfare card and a Cadillac."[23]

While recognizing the state of violence existing in El Salvador, the government maintains that refugee status is reserved for those who can prove that they have been individually singled out for political persecution. Simply to be victims of generalized violence is insufficient to mandate refugee status. Moreover, given the fact that Salvadorans and Guatemalans usually travel through Mexico and occasionally other Central American nations, where they could have stayed in safety, and given the historic patterns of substantial Salvadoran migration for economic purposes, these individuals are viewed as simply following in the footsteps of earlier waves of migrants. These were the principal stated reasons by the Office of the Coordinator of Refugee Affairs in proposing a Latin American refugee ceiling of only 1,000 individuals for FY 1984. The U.S. government provides considerable assistance to Central American refugees in the region, both through its own bilateral aid programs and through support of UNHCR assistance to the region. However, in the carefully reasoned arguments of the American Civil Liberties Union, U.S. assistance has not been sufficient to make these countries viable alternatives as places of refuge for all of the region's refugees. After describing the grim conditions for refugees in Central America and Mexico, the ACLU concludes "[i]n order for resettlement in Mexico or the countries of Central America to be a viable and humane option, the U.S. must make a substantial diplomatic and material commitment to the establishment of the clearest guarantees against involuntary repatriation and of safe and habitable conditions for Salvadorans in those countries."[24]

Most of the Central American refugees who make it to the United States are young, male, and reflecting their atypical mobility, probably better educated than those seeking refuge within the country or within the region.[25] According to officials providing direct services to the refugees, the Central Americans are also initially fearful and suspicious of others. They are terrified of being deported back to El Salvador and, given their experiences back home, are distrustful of authority and suspicious about what happens to information supplied to the U.S. government. In areas where there are substantial Salvadoran communities in the United States, the Salvadorans may be politicized for the first time. In talking with others from their own countries about their experiences, they may come to realize the extent of the violence within their homeland and in discussing such violence, turn to increasingly radical alternatives. Officials in several relief agencies noted the phenomenon of relatively apolitical young men developing a political consciousness through exposure to other Salvadorans in the United States. For Salvadorans and Guatemalans who end up residing in areas lacking such a sense of community, however, the principal characteristic of life may be not politicization through community, but isolation out of fear. Above all, the Salvadoran/Guatemalan fleeing violence fears being deported.

The Central Americans who come to the United States are not officially recognized as refugees under U.S. law. In fact, most of them have little contact—official or otherwise—with U.S. authorities. They typically come into the political arena only after being detained by immigration authorities for being in the country illegally. The Refugee Act of 1980 provides two very distinct processes for admitting individuals to the United States for reasons of political persecution: the refugee process (intended to be administered in the field and designed for relatively large numbers of people) and the political asylum process for those few individuals already in the United States who express well-founded fears about returning home. As outlined below, these two processes involve very different actors and very distinct procedures, although neither process recognizes the claims of Central Americans.

THE REFUGEE POLICYMAKING PROCESS

The number of refugees admitted to the United States is determined by "ceilings" established each year by the Office of the U.S. Coordinator for Refugee Affairs. The Coordinator emphasizes the fact that these are ceilings, not quotas. Table 6.2 presents the refugee ceilings for FY 1983 and 1984. In spite of the 90,000 ceiling in 1983 for refugees, only 60,000 to 62,000 were actually admitted, due primarily to lower than anticipated INS approval rates and the introduction of English language and cultural programs that temporarily slowed the flow of refugees.

Table 6.2: Refugee ceilings, FY 1983 and 1984, and estimated arrivals for FY 1983.

Region	Ceiling for 1983	Estimated arrivals FY 1983	Ceiling for FY 1984
Africa	3,000	2,700-2,800	3,000
E. Asia	64,000	37,000-38,000	50,000
E. Europe & USSR	15,000	14,500-15,000	12,000
Near East & South Asia	6,000	5,200-5,400	6,000
Latin America	2,000	600-800	1,000
TOTALS	90,000	60,000-62,000	72,000

Source: U.S. Coordinator for Refugee Affairs, *Proposed Refugee Admissions and Allocations for Fiscal Year 1984* (Washington, D.C.: Department of State), 18.

Thus, in the refugee process, the decision to admit refugees is made in accord with a specified set of priorities within a numerical guideline. Individuals are admitted as refugees within the context of general U.S. immigration law and are accepted only with a sponsor in order to encourage their adaptation to national life. Ideally the decision is made outside the United States, in order to ensure the orderly transfer of refugees.

Very few Salvadorans and Guatemalans have been admitted to the United States as refugees. Indeed in 1984 fewer than 300 Latin Americans were admitted as refugees—in contrast with 13,000 from Eastern Europe. As noted above, the U.S. government does not consider the Salvadorans leaving their countries to be refugees. They are considered to be economic migrants. The fact that Salvadorans (and Guatemalans to a lesser extent) are not admitted to the United States as refugees has meant that they have had no legal basis for entry into the country. So they come illegally, following patterns of migration established by a generation of Salvadorans coming to the United States in search of employment. Many Salvadorans are detained at the border while others are detained at their place of work, though an estimated two to five Salvadorans remain undetected for each one detained.

The issue of detention and deportation of Central Americans is a very controversial one.[26] Increased security at the border has resulted in an increase in apprehension of illegal aliens seeking entry. Ridgeway reports that the number of illegal aliens apprehended at the border increased from 750,000 to more than one million in 1983.[27] Estimates of the number of Salvadorans deported by the INS range from 500 to 1,000 per month.[28]

The question of the fate of the Salvadorans returned home (whether formally deported or "voluntarily" returned) is also an exceedingly controversial one. Before being returned to El Salvador, all Salvadorans are interviewed by the Salvadoran Consul General in Los Angeles. The State Department and the INS argue that there is absolutely no evidence that those Salvadorans returned home are the victims of the violence at a higher rate than those already there. Human rights and church groups dispute this argument, citing many cases in which deported Salvadorans have been tortured and killed.

Since few Central Americans have been awarded refugee status while thousands are apprehended for illegal entry into the United States, the number of Salvadorans applying for political asylum in the United States has increased dramatically—far beyond the numbers envisaged by the government when the Refugee Act of 1980 was passed.

The Refugee Act of 1980 established a policy by which individuals in the United States can be awarded political asylum if they are able to prove that they are victims of political persecution. Political asylum was intended for use by a limited number of individuals fleeing political persecution, but is currently being challenged by masses of Central Americans seeking protection through the asylum process. There is currently a backlog of over 100,000 applications for political asylum. In 1981 the INS processed only 5,000 applications and in 1982 only 11,000.[29] For the individual applying for political asylum, the process (with its appeals procedures) is a slow one. The Salvadoran applying for political asylum, even if his or her claim is denied, may be able to postpone deportation for several years while the claim is being processed. Critics charge, however, that "the normally slow processes of the Immigration and Naturalization Service are speeded up to return Salvadorans as quickly as possible."[30] And in fact, the INS has moved more quickly in the past two years.

Most of the Central Americans applying for political asylum do so only after having been apprehended for being in the country illegally. As workers in agencies servicing the refugees explain, the reasons for this delay are clear. The Central Americans are afraid to provide the necessary information to the U.S. government for fear that it will be used in El Salvador against their family, relatives, or acquaintances. Although the detailed information regarding political persecution is intended to be confidential, there are few guarantees that it will not be transmitted back to El Salvador and used by the security forces for their own purposes. Furthermore, the Central Americans in the United States illegally are aware that very few applications for political asylum are granted. Given the fact that the chance of a successful claim is so small (and the potential harm resulting from such a claim is so great), Central Americans in the United States illegally do not generally consider political asylum until they are faced with no other option—when they are detained and facing deportation.

From the government's perspective, the fact that most Central Americans do not apply for political asylum until they are about to be deported weakens their case. According to Duane Austin of the INS, the Central Americans might be presumed to have a stronger case if they declared their intention to seek political asylum immediately upon entering the country instead of waiting months or years until apprehended to file.[31]

The Refugee Act of 1980 requires a case-by-case settlement of all applications for asylum. Individuals applying for political asylum submit their applications to INS District Directors. When the District Director denies a case or does not hear the claim, the individual is placed in exclusion (if apprehended while trying to enter the United States) or deportation hearings (if apprehended while already in the country). During the proceedings the individual has a right to raise the question of political asylum before the presiding Immigration Judge. Individuals subject to exclusion proceedings may be detained pending an asylum decision at the discretion of the District Director. While this detention was usually waived in the past, since 1981 "[t]he Reagan administration has adopted a policy that requires the District Director to adhere to the requirement that all persons subject to exclusion be detained, except in emergency situations. In practice, this requirement affects—and is intended to affect —mainly Haitian boat people and Salvadorans who have crossed the U.S.-Mexico border."[32]

The burden of proof is on the individual who completes an application giving biographical information and information regarding his or her fear of persecution. Further information is then collected and the INS examining officer interviews the applicant to assess the credibility of the applicant and to add further information to the application. The completed application is sent to the Department of State's Bureau of Human Rights and Humanitarian Affairs (BHRHA) where a special asylum affairs section prepares an advisory opinion. This opinion is extremely important in determining the outcome of the case. The Bureau is asked to comment on the applicant's alleged fear of persecution based on its knowledge of conditions in a given country. Occasionally the U.S. embassy is asked to verify a particular incident (giving rise to the refugees' fears described above). The State Department's advisory opinion is usually adhered to by the INS District Director and the number of Salvadorans granted asylum is very low. In 1981, 2 Salvadorans were granted asylum (and 154 denied); in 1982, 74 were granted asylum (and 169 denied); in 1983, 230 were granted asylum (and approximately 4,000 denied). In 1984 the government granted 328 Salvadoran asylum claims and denied 13,045; only 3 Guatemalan asylum claims were accepted and 753 were denied. This stands in contrast with Nicaraguans (where 1,018 were accepted and 7,274 rejected) and Iranians (where 5,017 were accepted and 3,216 rejected).[33] The decision of the immigration judges may be appealed to the Board of Immigration Appeals (BIA) within the Department of Justice, which is independent of the INS. Statistics are not collected by nationality on the outcome of cases appealed.

The asylum process is slow and frustrates both those who feel that the Central Americans are being denied fair treatment and those within the government seeking a rational, controlled process. Governmental opposition to the current use of political asylum is widespread. As one INS official stated, "while the Salvadorans can stay in the U.S. for years while their cases are being appealed after entering the U.S. illegally, there are some 1.5 million individuals who have been awarded legal permission to emigrate to the U.S. who are waiting until there is room within the quota to come to the U.S. Some of them will wait 5 or 10 years before they come. What happens to them? The whole process is being subverted by the frivolous claims for asylum."[34]

In comparison with the refugee admissions process, the administration exercises much less control over the number of individuals who submit claims for asylum. As M. Heilman explains, there is absolutely no limit on the number of people who can be introduced into the asylum process, in spite of governmental ceilings for refugees. Furthermore, while an individual must meet general immigration requirements in order to be admitted as a refugee, he or she does not have to be admissible as an asylee and in fact most who are here do not meet U.S. immigration standards. No sponsor is needed for asylum claims. While the refugee process ensures definitive rulings, the would-be asylee has a whole "play of administrative and judicial processes which will assure that his claim gets more attention than that envisioned by the people writing the Refugee Act."[35] While the determination to grant refugee status is discretionary, the asylum process—which takes twice as long and is coupled with the withholding of deportation—limits the government's discretionary powers.[36]

This examination of the refugee and asylum processes has demonstrated that very few Central Americans are admitted to the United States because of their political persecution. Together the refugee and asylum procedures limit to a few hundred the Central Americans who are permitted to enter the United States legally. UN investigators who criticized the U.S. procedures concluded that "there is a systematic practice designed to forcibly return Salvadorans irrespective of the rights of their asylum claim."[37] They have urged the INS to take actions to change the process. Currently in the United States, various groups are working to change U.S. admissions procedures for Central American refugees, through use of extended voluntary departure status and through civil disobedience in the sanctuary movement.

Extended voluntary departure (EVD) is a practice that has been used to give temporary protection to individuals from areas in a state of turmoil and danger. In the past, individuals from some 20 countries have been eligible for EVD, including those from Uganda, Iran, and Poland. The DeConcini/Moakley bill currently in Congress would prohibit the U.S. government from deporting Salvadorans for at least two years while a study is conducted on the fate of those who have been deported. When the General Accounting Office certifies that conditions have improved, then the Salvadorans may be forced to return home. While this bill would certainly provide safe haven for thousands of Salvadorans currently living in the U.S. illegally, the bill is quite restrictive in that it applies only to Salvadorans (and not to Guatemalans) currently living in the U.S. Clearly the government is afraid that passage of a more inclusive bill would serve as a magnet for Central America's "feet people."

In 1982 a group of clergy and lay people from Tucson started what was to become a national grassroots movement of providing protection to Central American refugees by declaring public sanctuary to shelter Central American refugees.[38] Tracing their roots to Biblical practices and to English common law, the U.S. churches declared their protection of the refugees in defiance of U.S. immigration law. In fact many sanctuary leaders argued that what they were seeking was application of existing U.S. law. They maintain that currently the Refugee Act of 1980 is not being applied in a fair and equitable manner—as was intended by its drafters. By offering protection to the refugees they seek to bring the issue of the refugees and the larger issues of U.S. policies in Central America to the attention of the U.S. public. Currently over 300 churches and other groups are offering sanctuary to Central American refugees with the active participation of 50,000 to 100,000 church people. The INS has consistently maintained that these individuals are breaking the law by harboring illegal aliens. As the movement grew in strength, the INS professed little interest in arresting sanctuary workers or in violating church property to find and deport Central American refugees. In 1984, however, several church workers were arrested in Texas while transporting Salvadoran refugees. The church workers were charged with transportation of illegal aliens and conspiracy to transport illegal aliens. Throughout the lengthy judicial process, the U.S. workers maintained that they were acting out of religious conviction in providing sanctuary to the refugees. However, several of the workers have received prison sentences.

In January 1985, 16 sanctuary workers were indicted after a secret grand jury in Phoenix heard some of the 100 tapes made by the INS in its 10-month investigation of the sanctuary movement. Sixty refugees were arrested and named as unindicted co-conspirators in Phoenix, Tucson, Seattle, Philadelphia, and Rochester. Although the arrests were unexpected, even more alarming to individuals involved in the movement was the extent to which the INS had gone in investigating the sanctuary network. INS agents had infiltrated the "Underground Railroad," had made secret tape recordings, and paid informers for information about the movement. In spite of the government's crackdown, the sanctuary movement seems determined to continue its mission of aiding the victims of Central America's violence. In fact many see the government's crackdown as directly related to U.S. foreign policies in the region. Yet the politicized nature of the debate over U.S. refugee policies is not new. For years, critics have decried the politicized application of U.S. refugee law to those seeking admission to the United States. U.S. refugee policy has always reflected U.S. foreign policy objectives as well as competition between bureaucracies within the government.

As in the case of the other governments examined here, U.S. policy toward the Central American refugees is clearly shaped by national foreign policy objectives. More than any of the other governments, however, U.S. policy toward the refugees has been consistent with its foreign policies toward Central America. The U.S. government is more concerned with the victims of the Nicaraguan (and Cuban) governments than with those of governments supported by the U.S. And in fact the government views refugee policy as an explicit tool for implementing U.S. foreign policies. Thus when Secretary of State George Schultz was asked whether, if CIA-backed Nicaraguan *contras* suffered military reverses, U.S. forces would "save their skins?" he replied, "well if they seek to leave someplace and want asylum or something like that, well, they may come here."[39]

With respect to the Salvadorans, U.S. foreign policy makes it imperative that they not be admitted as refugees. As many authors have noted "[f]or the State Department to recommend asylum or authorize an 'EVD' [extended voluntary departure] status for Salvadorans here would be to admit explicitly that the government of El Salvador, which the U.S. firmly supports, is responsible for the conditions which have caused their mass exodus."[40] Furthermore the use of refugee policy as a tool of foreign policy is evident in administration projections of a massive outpouring of refugees should the leftists win a victory in El Salvador. President Reagan in June 1983 warned of a "tidal wave of refugees swarming into our country" if leftist movements in Central America are successful.[41] And Williams reports that an unnamed NSC staffer in addressing hispanic evangelical leaders warned them that "[a]n influx from Latin America of 8 million refugees seeking jobs and homes would cost the country in excess of $115 billion—but the cost goes beyond dollars to the democratic and social problems it would cause, the destruction of the economic recovery. . . . The human costs are incalculable."[42] The specter of millions of refugees from Central America is thus used to mobilize public opinion in support of U.S. policy in Central America.

While U.S. foreign policy objectives under the Reagan administration thus favor restrictive policies toward Central American refugees, different groups within the U.S. government have different concerns. The Office of the U.S. Coordinator for Refugee Affairs represents the administration's views in carrying out its mandated responsibility of coordinating U.S. policy toward refugees. The coordinator (currently Eugene Douglas) is responsible for representing the government's perspective in annual consultations with Congress. The Coordinator's Office is thus beset with contradictory pressures—to coordinate refugee policy and thus presumably to serve as an advocate for refugees, and at the same time to represent the administration's restrictive policies. This ambivalence in function is reflected in the fact that the Coordinator has offices both in the State Department and in the Old Executive Office Building. Douglas has supported lower ceilings and lower budgets for refugee-related programs and favored cutting the time period during which refugees can receive aid from 36 to 18 months.[43] Although reportedly very sympathetic to Indochinese refugees and with a particular interest in Thailand, Douglas has shown little interest in Central America. While visiting refugee camps in Honduras he reportedly brushed off the concerns of workers of international voluntary agencies, saying he had seen much worse.[44] While the concerns of the Coordinator mandate a restrictive policy toward the refugees, other offices within the State Department are concerned with issues of U.S. compliance with international law and with providing aid to refugees around the world.

Refugee Programs (RP) administers the State Department's refugee programs and is responsible for developing and implementing policies and programs related to refugee assistance overseas. By working on behalf of those formally recognized as refugees, their efforts are largely concentrated in other countries. In Central America, they work closely with the governments of nations hosting large numbers of refugees. They are also responsible for setting priorities for admission of refugees to the U.S. and for providing resources for their reception and placement in U.S. communities through cooperative arrangements with voluntary agencies. About 35 percent of RP's 1982 budget was spent on U.S.-related activities, the remainder in other countries.[45] Personnel working within RP tend to be more sympathetic to the plight of the Central American refugees than are officials with different constituencies.

The Bureau for Human Rights and Humanitarian Affairs (BHRHA), also within the State Department, is responsible for issuing the advisory opinions that are so crucial in asylum cases. Again, reflecting the administration's desire for consistency, the evaluation of the BHRHA has been that conditions in El Salvador do not warrant extending refugee status to those coming to the United States. While officials in RP are aiding the victims of the Central American violence in Central America, the BHRHA consistently advises against granting political asylum to victims in the United States. The divergent interests and concerns of these two programs are reflected in their different policy orientations.

N. L. Zucker describes the State Department's concern with refugee issues as characterized by considerable shuffling of administrative apparatus and personnel. High turnover in refugee-related programs is the result of foreign service officers' perceptions that refugee work hampers their career advancement. This high turnover has resulted in poor institutional memory. Zucker further argues that the State Department has done little significant contingency planning, has inadequately evaluated domestic programs, and has not monitored voluntary agency performance.[46]

The interests represented by the Immigration and Naturalization Service involve questions of economic well-being and security in its efforts to enforce immigration policy and to patrol the border. The INS is concerned with implementing the immigration laws in a fair and impartial manner. As an INS spokesman explained,[47] "our relationship with a country is not supposed to play a role in granting asylum although there will be higher acceptability rates from countries with histories of persecution than countries beset by turmoil. I know of no instances in which we are not following the law." From the INS perspective, Congress did not intend to respond to the needs of all the world's victims of revolution and civil war, but rather to aid those individuals fleeing persecution. The INS favors policies giving the government greater control over refugee admissions and the power to rationalize policies toward refugees in terms of general immigration issues. The INS particularly resents the politicization of the refugee policy-making process. Congressional resolutions to extend EVD status to Salvadorans are viewed as violating the separation of powers, and the efforts of individual Congressmen on behalf of specific Central Americans are resented by the INS. But the INS, in spite of its mandate to impartially implement national laws, is also affected by political concerns. As long as the Reagan administration favors restricted admission of Central Americans, the INS will pay relatively little attention to non-binding congressional resolutions.

Currently the State Department and the INS are working in tandem: both support restrictive Central American migration policies. But this has not always been the case. During the massive influx of Indochinese refugees, the INS and the State Department were often locked in bitter controversy as the INS sought to limit the numbers of refugees admitted while the State Department favored a more liberal admissions policy.[48]

While the INS is concerned about the impact of refugee migrations on general economic well-being of the country, the Office of Refugee Resettlement (ORR) within the Department of Health and Human Services is the agency with chief operational responsibility for domestic assistance to refugees. ORR, in accord with procedures established by the Refugee Act of 1980, coordinates programs and distributes funds to state and local communities involved with refugee resettlement. Recent administrative changes (in which the ORR apparatus developed slowly and was transferred from the Secretary's Office to the Office of the Social Security Administration) and significant budget cuts have diminished ORR's power.

The issue of the refugees has a legal dimension as well. The fact that all individuals in the United States have a right to appeal asylum decisions to the courts has introduced yet another element into the refugee policy-making arena, an element which the executive has not been able to control. Questions about the protection of the civil rights of the refugees as well as questions about the interpretation and application of U.S. law are central to the issue of refugee policy. The fact that the courts can act—and have acted—in opposition to U.S. policy has meant a further check on executive power in this area. For example, while the State Department has consistently viewed the Haitians arriving in the United States as economic migrants, in 1980 Judge James L. King ruled that the poverty from which the Haitians were fleeing was a political condition. In clear contradiction to the State Department, he ruled that the Haitians were thus eligible for admission to the United States as refugees under the 1980 Refugee Act.[49] In 1984 a federal court in California ruled that individuals persecuted for not having taken a political stand in El Salvador were eligible for political asylum, as neutrality in El Salvador could constitute grounds for persecution.

Within the government each agency—with its own set of interests and objectives—seeks to maximize its institutional power and influence. The election of Ronald Reagan in 1980 and the subsequent development of more restrictive refugee policies created a climate in which personal career advancement as well as institutional prestige and power depended on implementing governmental policies. For individual foreign service officers, there is little to be gained from working too hard on behalf of refugees. The emphasis within the State Department has shifted from the human rights of the Carter administration to the anti-communism of the Reagan administration. Clearly refugees—at least from noncommunist countries—have a much less significant role to play in confronting communism than in implementing human rights.

U.S. policies toward the Central American refugees are shaped by these competing bureaucratic and political interests. While the State Department and INS seek to limit Central American refugee admissions in order to support U.S. foreign policy objectives and immigration concerns, administration critics view the refugees as evidence of the failure of U.S. policies in that region. Church and human rights groups are becoming increasingly active on Central America generally and see in the refugee issue a way of generating public awareness and concern about the Central American revolutions and U.S. policy toward Central America. Various hispanic groups have focused primarily on issues relating to immigration policy generally and on the far larger migration of undocumented workers. However, given the growing political clout of hispanic groups, the increasing politicization of refugee issues, and expanding congressional involvement in the process, it is likely that the question of U.S. policy toward the Central American refugees will be increasingly addressed in partisan political terms.

U.S. POLICY ASSESSED

U.S. policies toward the Central American refugees are the product of a variety of competing pressures. While the United Nations, and America's heritage as a nation of refuge, push the government toward generous admissions policies, other influences mitigate against this pressure. The U.S. government under the Reagan administration has repeatedly shown itself to be less concerned with international norms and public opinion than under previous administrations. The U.S. invasion of Grenada and U.S. refusal to be bound by World Court decisions in cases brought by Nicaragua are evidence of this. At the same time, high unemployment has given rise to isolationist pressures to keep foreigners out. The fear of being inundated by thousands of desperate, low-paid Central Americans has been used by the government in justifying its restrictive policies toward the refugees.

Analysis of the determinants of U.S. refugee policies reveals a multitude of competing pressures that have resulted in restrictive policies that give *de facto* preference to those individuals able to make the long clandestine journey to the United States and to live here illegally once they arrive. A more open policy would probably result in more women and children migrating to the United States and consequently in higher governmental costs. Furthermore the restrictive admissions policy ensures a relatively quiet population of refugees, as the costs of speaking out are very high (although some refugees, of course, have been very vocal in opposing administration policies). The closed admissions policy further limits the number of refugees coming to the country. Clearly governmental policy makers are concerned with the impact of extending refugee or EVD status to Salvadorans. As one congressional staffer explained, "if we legalize the presence of the half million Salvadorans who are already here, how many more millions will come?"[50]

The process of formulating rational, consistent, and humane policies toward refugees is difficult precisely because competing political and bureaucratic interests are involved. But it is also difficult because of the moral issues involved. Given the fact that there are thousands of desperate people outside the borders of the United States—victims of hunger, disease, and calamities—the question of deciding to give preference to victims of *political* persecution over other types of tragic circumstances implies a moral judgment. A moral choice is also involved in deciding which of the deserving millions to admit and to aid. In spite of its wealth, the United States has finite resources; decisions to use those resources to aid a particular group always mean that others will not be aided.[51]

After briefly discussing the refugee policies of other governments toward the Central American refugees, the concluding chapter draws comparisons between the cases examined here.

7

Conclusions

While most Central American refugees have sought safety in Mexico, Costa Rica, Honduras, and the United States, smaller numbers have sought protection in Nicaragua, other Central American nations, and Canada. After briefly surveying the policies of those governments toward the refugees, this concluding chapter addresses some of the common themes in refugee policy making.

NICARAGUA: THE POLITICS OF WELCOME

Nicaraguan policies toward the Central American refugees are shaped by the political orientations of the regime and by the nation's experience during its 1978/79 revolution. An estimated 100,000 to 200,000 Nicaraguans sought refuge from the violence during the last two years of the Somoza regime.[1] Another 800,000 Nicaraguans were internally displaced. In fact, the Costa Rican government not only provided refuge to the Nicaraguans fleeing the political violence, but it also became a center for the political exile community to lead the armed struggle against Somoza. Without the support of the Costa Rican government (and to a lesser extent other governments in the region), the revolutionary struggle in Nicaragua would have been much more difficult.[2] Consequently, the Nicaraguan government has not only supported the Salvadoran revolutionary struggle, but has developed liberal policies toward the refugees produced by that struggle.

In March 1980 Nicaragua acceded to both the 1951 UN convention relating to the status of refugees and to the 1967 protocol. Shortly thereafter large numbers of Salvadorans began to arrive, at first by ferry across the Gulf of Fonseca and later over land through Honduras. Most of the refugees seeking sanctuary in Nicaragua are Salvadoran peasants although there are several hundred Guatemalans as well as political exiles from throughout the region.[3]

In August 1980 the government designated the Ministry of Social Welfare (now the Nicaraguan Institute of Social Security and Welfare) as the governmental agency responsible for carrying out refugee assistance activities. Coordination and implementation of aid programs is handled by the National Office of Refugees. The UNHCR works closely with the Nicaraguan government and with nongovernmental organizations in serving the needs of the refugees who come. In the past three years, the UNHCR has provided $5 million in assistance to the refugees. Currently there are approximately 18,000 refugees in Nicaragua (17,500 from El Salvador and 500 from Guatemala), a number that has remained stable for the past year.

The refugees who arrive in Nicaragua go first to special transit or reception centers at León, Estelí, and Chinandega, where they stay for a period ranging from a few weeks to a few months. They are then moved into rural settlements where they can become self-sufficient in food production. Six cooperatives have been started and are designed to service both the refugees as well as Nicaraguan families, in an effort to increase the refugees' integration into national life. By virtually all accounts the majority of refugees have settled easily into Nicaraguan life. In fact, according to a recent report by the UNHCR, as of September 1984 less than 2,000 received aid from the UNHCR and most of those are in the process of being integrated into cooperatives.[4]

The report of an official Canadian fact-finding commission concluded that Nicaragua is the most favored destination of new refugees from El Salvador and Guatemala. Educated exiles not comfortable in Nicaragua usually go to Mexico.[5] The official policy of the Nicaraguan government toward the refugees is the most generous in the region. The Sandinista government fully recognizes the Central American arrivals as refugees and accords them full freedom to live, travel, and work in the country. They have the same civil rights as Nicaraguan citizens to education and health care. The main difficulties facing the refugees are economic. Given the state of the Nicaraguan economy, jobs are hard to find and governmental financial support for the refugees is limited. Furthermore, refugees seeking asylum in Nicaragua face considerable political difficulties back home. Once the individual refugee has lived in Nicaragua, he or she may find mobility to other Central American nations limited. The political repercussions back home may be serious as refugees who choose to live in Nicaragua may confirm governmental suspicions of their leftist orientations. However the U.S. State Department reports that in 1983 about 4,000 Salvadorans returned home from Nicaragua.[6]

Nicaragua's welcoming posture toward the Salvadoran refugees (and toward a growing number of Guatemalans) is consistent with its foreign policy of support for revolutionary movements in the region as well as its growing isolation from the other governments of the area. Even with its current economic difficulties, it would be hard for the Sandinista regime to justify restrictionist policies toward the refugees. The nation's own historical experience—where more than half the nation's population was forced to flee their homes—and its ideological opposition to the repressive regimes of El Salvador and Guatemala mandate an open, generous policy toward the refugees. Supporting the refugees confirms Sandinista support for revolutionary movements in the eyes of the Central American governments and the United States, and this may contribute to Nicaragua's political difficulties with those countries. Thus Nicaragua pays a political price for its welcoming policies toward the Central American refugees.

CANADA: DISTANT WELCOME

Canada has become a country of first asylum for refugees from throughout the world and today many Central Americans look to Canada as a safe haven. From 1981 to 1983 some 1,200 Salvadorans were settled in Canada through governmental programs. In recent years the Canadian government has been quite generous in accepting Salvadoran refugees; certainly in comparison with the United States, the Canadians have extended refugee status to many more individuals. However Canada has also not experienced the waves of Central American refugees that the United States has experienced. Historically, as G. E. Dirks points out, the Canadian government has viewed Latin America as a preserve of the United States and has been relatively indifferent to Latin American migration.[7] In terms of its political culture, Canada has seen itself not as a place of temporary refuge for victims of political violence but as a country for permanent resettlement. Indeed that was the Canadian experience.

This worldview of distance from Latin America changed in 1973 with the violent overthrow of Salvador Allende. "While the Canadian government initially moved slowly to establish a refugee admissions programme, pressure from Members of Parliament, organized labour, and a number of humanitarian organizations including the churches, ultimately resulted in Canada accepting approximately 7,000 refugees from Chile for permanent resettlement between 1974 and 1977."[8]

In terms of its foreign policy, Canada has been reluctant to become actively involved in the Central American conflict, again seeing this as an area inappropriate for its diplomatic initiatives. Initially, the Canadian government focused its attention on admitting individual refugees in danger of being forcibly repatriated to their country of origin and was reluctant to develop a special category of admissions for Central Americans. However, due to domestic political pressure, the Canadian government has expanded its refugee admissions target figure from 1,000 Latin American refugees in 1982 to 4,000 in 1985. The churches have been particularly active in pressing for higher Central American refugee admissions. Recently, many nongovernmental organizations expressed concern about Canadian differential treatment of Salvadoran and Guatemalan refugees.

While Canada professes to be a country of refuge, the government has not hesitated to impose visa requirements whenever there is a significant inflow of migrants from a particular country into Canada. This means that the airlines will not transport individuals without a visa. In the past this has occurred in cases such as Chile, Haiti, India, Sri Lanka, and Peru. A recent decision to require visas for Guatemalans was viewed by many nongovernmental organizations as an effort to restrict Central American refugee admissions[9] and to deny Central Americans access to the appeals procedure available to refugee claimants in Canada.

In comparison with the United States, Canadian policies toward the refugees seem much more open. Many Central Americans have been awarded refugee status by the Canadian government after having been turned down by the U.S. government. However Canada—as a country physically far removed from the violence—has never been forced to respond to the plight of hundreds of thousands of individuals desperately seeking sanctuary. Given Canada's current economic difficulties, Canada's welcoming posture may be at least in part a function of its distance from the refugee-producing areas.

OTHER COUNTRIES: ISOLATED PROJECTS

There are several other countries with smaller numbers of Central Americans. The governments of these countries have generally supported specific projects for aiding the refugees without formulating comprehensive policies.

Currently a large (but undetermined) number of Salvadorans are living in Guatemala without UNHCR supervision. A voluntary organization, the ACJ (Association Chretienne de Jeunes), began aid programs to the Salvadoran refugees in Guatemala in October 1983 and currently the UNHCR supplies some financial aid through the ACJ. The Salvadorans living in Guatemala face serious problems of insecurity and fear of expulsion. As many plan to emigrate to Canada, they are uninterested in becoming settled in Guatemala.[10] Obviously, given the repressive nature of the Guatemalan government, Salvadorans seeking protection in Guatemala do so at great risk. The lack of opportunities to visit Guatemala have prevented nongovernmental organizations from independently verifying the situation of the refugees there.

Belize is a country in historic and cultural opposition to Guatemala. Guatemala's territorial claims and military threats to Belize have created considerable fear on the part of the Belizean authorities about Guatemalan intentions. Culturally, Belize's population is dominated by English-speaking blacks; politically, the Belize government has tried to remain isolated from the region's conflicts. While Guatemalan peasants have historically migrated to Belize in search of employment, beginning in 1981 several thousand Salvadorans came to Belize in search of refuge. The 2,000 or so refugees place heavy burdens on the governmental and economic infrastructure of the country. As a small nation (only 140,000 inhabitants) Belize is currently struggling with the same problems of formulating economic policies to meet the needs of its citizens at the same time as they develop the political institutions of a newly independent government. In this context of a regime struggling with state-building, even small numbers of refugees have had a substantial impact. Most significantly, the presence of Spanish-speaking Central American refugees threatens to change the nation's ethnic balance.

While there is some resentment of the Salvadoran refugees, by and large, the Belizean government has responded quite generously. In 1984 the government issued an amnesty decree, legalizing the situation of aliens, particularly Guatemalan and Salvadoran refugees, who entered Belize illegally before May 1, 1984. In 1982, the government donated 15,000 acres of fertile land to establish an agricultural settlement for both Salvadoran and Belizean families. With financial assistance from the UNHCR and administrative assistance from the Mennonite Central Committee, this Valley of Peace project is designed for 140-150 Salvadoran families and 50-60 Belizeans. The Belizean Ministry of Defense and Home Affairs has overall responsibility for the refugees.[11]

There are other specific UNHCR projects for the Central American refugees in other countries. For example, programs in Panama have been set up to respond to the needs of approximately 1,000 Salvadoran refugees in Panama. Both rural projects (such as the settlement at Ciudad Romero) and urban self-sufficiency projects are currently under way, again with financial support from UNHCR. The Ministry of Home Affairs and Justice holds the responsibility for all refugee matters in the country.

While projects for the Central American refugees are in operation in a dozen or so countries, most of the refugees continue to seek protection in Costa Rica, Mexico, Honduras, and the United States. It is those countries that have been the most severely affected by the refugee migrations.

CAUSES AND CONSEQUENCES OF THE POLITICS OF REFUGE

The present exodus of refugees is due not only to specific political events in the refugees' countries of origin, but to mounting ethnic conflicts and to the changing nature of political violence in the region.

In a perceptive essay on ethnicity as a refugee-generating process, Jason Clay notes that Third World governments have traditionally faced monumental problems in trying to incorporate diverse ethnic groups into their national political institutions.[12] The need to establish national identities and to foster loyalty to a new state has been used in regions throughout the world as justification for one-party authoritarian rule. Such rule almost inevitably leads to the adoption of measures that restrict the freedom of the ethnic groups. In the case of Central America, the Miskitus' flight from what they perceived as ethnic persecution and the documented violence by the Guatemalan government directed explicitly at indigenous populations are cases where ethnic conflict has clearly produced refugee migrations. Moreover, in both cases the presence of ethnic groups marginal to the national government has caused governments to see demands for preservation of indigenous culture as challenges to their power. As the governments come to realize that the primary loyalty of their indigenous populations is not to the institutions of the state but to community institutions, they become suspicious of their activities. The regimes correctly perceive that their enemies—whether *contras* or revolutionaries—can use this ethnic dissatisfaction as a tool against the government itself. As the government moves to restrict these opportunities, whether by relocating the indigenous groups or by forcing them to demonstrate their loyalty to the government through participation in civilian patrols, conflict increases and members of the indigenous groups seek protection outside national borders when possible.

This process of ethnic conflict is intensified by economic scarcity. As economic conditions worsen, "dominant groups expand into the traditional areas of less powerful groups" and "increase their penetration into more isolated areas where remote groups have often lived in relative autonomy."[13]

Ethnic conflicts, then, exacerbated by both the growth of national revolutionary movements and growing economic hardships, are a major cause of Central American refugee migrations. The process of seeking refuge, not only beyond the traditional area of indigenous settlement but outside the national borders as well, has changed—probably irreversibly changed—the nature of the indigenous communities. Changing values, language, and exposure to different lifestyles will undoubtedly serve as a force for cultural change in the indigenous communities.

A second major cause of the refugee migrations, as discussed in Chapter 2, is the changing nature of political violence. With the growth of revolutionary movements challenging the status quo dominated by elitist politics, governments have responded by penetrating the countryside and by pressuring the civilian populations to demonstrate their loyalty to the government. In the cities, campaigns of terror have produced similar results: the displacement of many civilian noncombatants who had not been previously involved in politics. Throughout Central America—and throughout the Third World generally—the growing incorporation of civilian populations into political conflicts has led to an increase in refugees fleeing these political conflicts, and to increased problems for the governments that host them.

The countries hosting large numbers of Central American refugees are quite varied, from the wealthy United States to debt-ridden Honduras, and from democratic Costa Rica to authoritarian Mexico. Differing governmental capabilities and foreign policy objectives have produced different policies toward the refugees, as have differences in the scope and nature of these refugee situations. Although the responses have been disparate, several common themes emerge from the comparative analysis of refugee policy making.

One of the reasons the Central American refugees have caused so many problems for the host governments is that national laws and processes designed for processing individual cases of asylum were simply inadequate for responding to the Central Americans. All of the governments had to develop policies in response to a fundamentally different sort of refugee than those political exiles who had come before. In none of the countries was there any preparation or any forewarning that the countries were about to be overwhelmed by masses of refugees seeking protection. The United States was the only country with experience in mass refugee migrations, with the Cuban influxes of the early 1960s, the Indochinese boatpeople of 1979, and the Mariel exodus in 1981.

For all of the countries the formulation of policies toward the Central American refugees has been a highly politicized matter. Refugee policy is clearly and unambiguously shaped by the foreign policy objectives of the regime. This has been particularly evident in the fact that refugees from different countries are accorded different treatment depending on the nature of relations between the governments of the sending and the receiving countries. The Honduran government treats refugees from

Nicaragua and from El Salvador differently, as does the U.S. government. Costa Rica's efforts at neutrality have been characterized by vacillation, and this inconsistency in foreign policy is paralleled by differential perceptions of the motives of the Salvadoran and Nicaraguan refugees. The single most important factor determining policies toward the refugees is a government's foreign policy toward the conflicts in Central America.

One of the important factors in the development of refugee policies in Mexico, Costa Rica, and Honduras is the influence of the U.S. government. The economic dependence of the countries—particularly at a time when all three are struggling with mammoth foreign debts—has made them more "attentive" to U.S. wishes. The U.S. government has made its Central American foreign policy objectives abundantly clear to the governments in the region. When coupled with limited economic resources and growing popular resentment of foreigners, all three governments have moved to restrict admissions of Salvadoran and Guatemalan refugees.

For all of the countries, relations with bordering countries have proven to be especially difficult. With the exception of the U.S.-Mexican frontier, national borders are located in deep jungles with inadequate transportation networks for effective national control of immigration. The remoteness of the regions and historical animosities between neighboring countries has meant that refugees from neighboring countries have been treated more cautiously than those coming from farther away.

In comparing the governments hosting large numbers of Central American refugees, there are clear differences in the processes by which refugee policies are formulated. Most obviously, the governmental unit encharged with formulating refugee policy varies markedly between countries. While in Mexico, responsibility for refugee policy is primarily in the domain of the Ministry of the Interior, the Foreign Relations Ministry is an active participant (although usually on the losing side) in that process. In Costa Rica, the Minister of Justice is the principal institutional actor in refugee policy. In Honduras the Minister of Defense plays the dominant role, whereas in Nicaragua, it is the Social Security Institute. And in the United States the INS and the State Department work together in formulating policy toward the refugees. Personalist influences on policy making are, however, important in all of the countries analyzed.

The UNHCR plays an important coordinating and unobtrusive political role. There is an inverse relationship between the influence of the UNHCR in a country and national economic and political capability. The more powerful and independent the country, the less influence exerted by the UNHCR. The UNHCR's main sources of power are the financial resources it makes available to governments and the moral power of an international organization with the weight of the United Nations behind it. Governments with substantial alternative sources of financial support and with the lesser concern for world opinion that comes with greater economic and political power are less likely to be influenced by the UNHCR. The most effective exercise of UNHCR power seems to be in its efforts to foster cooperation between the relevant agencies within the host government. Both Mexico's COMAR and Costa Rica's COMPARE owe much to UNHCR influence.

The presence of the Central American refugees both reflects and encourages the internationalization of the violence in Central America. International actors have sought to use the refugees for political purposes, as in the case of the *contras* and the Miskitus. The presence of the refugees inevitably complicates relations between the governments of bordering nations. Certainly relations have become more complicated between all of the bordering countries because of the refugees. The presence of the refugees has also made it more difficult to resolve outstanding conflicts between nations.

A further consequence of refugee migrations has been the growing awareness and involvement of the public in foreign policy issues. When refugees pour across a nation's borders with their tales of governmental torture and brutality, popular opposition to that government can increase. Whether in the United States, with the sanctuary movement making many American citizens acutely and personally aware of the violence occurring in Central America, or with the Nicaraguan refugees confirming the Costa Rican public's stereotypes of the Sandinista regime, the refugees are further publicizing the Central American conflicts. They are also personalizing the conflict and turning foreign policy concerns into domestic political issues. The lines between foreign and domestic policy have become fuzzy and less clear-cut as a result of the refugee migrations. At times reaction to refugees—particularly those coming from a country traditionally hostile to the host country—has been difficult for the host government trying to formulate coherent policies toward the refugees.

The refugee migrations from Central America and the pattern of governmental responses to those migrations show a changing conception of national sovereignty. What does sovereignty or even a national border mean in an era of mass migration? In all of the countries analyzed here, governmental officials have used exactly the same words to describe the impact of the refugees. They all say that their governments are "losing control of their borders." This feeling of having lost control over perhaps the most basic component of national sovereignty results in blame on foreigners, particularly immigrants, for domestic problems. It also has given rise to disenchantment with one's own government for failure to uphold national integrity.

The nations of Central America, Mexico, and the United States are becoming increasingly interdependent. Not only do political events in one country have a dramatic impact on politics in another, but now they can have an effect on a nation's economy and even on its culture by affecting the makeup of its very population. In fact, it may be possible to view all of these countries as part of a single system in which tensions in one part of the system are transferred to another through migration of refugees. This process of release of tension through production of refugee flows has been extensively studied in the context of economic migration,[14] but analysis of the Central American case would seem to indicate its relevance for understanding patterns of politically-motivated migration as well. If national borders could be controlled and the refugees kept out, the impact on national politics would be enormous. If El Salvador's borders were sealed and the 10 percent of its population now living abroad forced to return home, then we would see far higher casualties and possibly much more rapid political change as the pressure built to unsustainable levels. Refugee migrations may act as a safety valve in high pressure situations.

But for the present, the refugees continue to come out of the violence-stricken countries of the region. While the flood of refugees in the early 1980s has slowed to a trickle by 1985 due to the greater military capability of governments to prevent them from leaving, they will continue to come as long as violence and terror characterize their homelands. And so they arrive in host countries that do not want them and complicate still further an already complex web of international and intra-national relations. Not until there are fundamental political changes in the region and the root causes of the refugee migrations are addressed will the flow of refugees stop. Meanwhile, neither the countries that produce the refugees nor those that receive them will ever be the same.

Notes

CHAPTER 1

1. Washington *Post* (April 22, 1983), A13.
2. In contrast with this narrow definition of refugee status, the Organization of African Unity (OAU) in 1969 developed a broader definition of refugees to include those individuals displaced by generalized conditions of violence.
3. Astri Suhrke, "Global refugee movements and strategies of response," in Mary M. Kritz, ed., *U.S. Immigration and Refugee Policy* (Lexington, MA: Lexington Books, 1983).
4. Suhrke, "Global refugee movements."
5. Personal interview reported in Elizabeth G. Ferris, "Refugees and world politics: An overview," in Elizabeth G. Ferris, ed., *Refugees and World Politics* (New York: Praeger, 1985).

CHAPTER 2

1. Guy Poitras, "Through the revolving door: Central American manpower in the United States," *InterAmerican Economic Affairs* 36, No. 4 (Spring 1983), 63-78.
2. Adolfo Aguilar Zinser, "Mexico and the Guatemalan crisis," in Richard R. Fagen and Olga Pellicer, eds., *The Future of Central America: Policy Choices for the U.S. and Mexico* (Stanford, CA: Stanford Univ. Press, 1983), 164-67.
3. Walter LaFeber, *Inevitable Revolutions: The United States in Central America* (New York: W. W. Norton and Co., 1984), 184.
4. *Ibid.*, 175.
5. Atle Grahl-Madsen, *The Status of Refugees in International Law* 2 (Netherlands: A. W. Sitjtshoff, 1972), 46-66.
6. International Commission of Jurists, *The Application in Latin America of International Declarations and Conventions Relating to Asylum* (Geneva: International Commission of Jurists, 1975), 85.
7. Dennis Gallagher, "United States refugee policy and Latin America," *Refugee Policy Group Research Report* (Washington, D.C.: Refugee Policy Group, February 1983), 19.
8. Adolfo Perez Esquivel, "Interview," *Refugees* 22 (Oct. 1983).
9. Gallagher, "United States Refugee Policy," 18-20.
10. U.S. Congress House Committee on Foreign Affairs, "Briefing on the growing refugee problem: Implications for international organizations," Hearings before the subcommittee on International Organizations (Washington, D.C.: Government Printing Office, June 5, 1979), 55.
11. For a discussion of the Nicaraguan insurrection, see John A. Booth, *The End and the Beginning: The Nicaraguan Revolution* (Boulder, CO: Westview, 1982), and Thomas W. Walker, ed., *Nicaragua in Revolution* (New York: Praeger, 1982).
12. The initial difficulties of the Sandinista government in consolidating the revolution have been extensively discussed. See, for example, Booth, *The End and the Beginning*, and Walker, *Nicaragua in Revolution*.
13. *Inter-Hemispheric Education Resource Bulletin*, 2, No. 1 (Spring 1985), 3.

14. Jennie K. Lincoln, "Central America: Regional security issues," in Jennie K. Lincoln and Elizabeth G. Ferris, eds., *The Dynamics of Latin American Foreign Policies: Challenge for the 1980s* (Boulder, CO: Westview, 1984).

15. "Into the fray: Facts on the U.S. military in Central America," *The Defense Monitor* 13, No. 3 (1984), 10.

16. Jason W. Clay, "Ethnicity: Powerful factor in refugee flows," *World Refugee Survey 1984* (New York: U.S. Committee for Refugees, 1984), 10-16.

17. David Brown, *El Salvador: la Tierra y el Hombre* (San Salvador: Ministerio de Educación, 1975).

18. Cynthia Arnson, *El Salvador: A Revolution Confronts the United States* (Washington, D.C.: Institute for Policy Studies, 1982), 7.

19. Tom Barry, Beth Wood, and Deb Preusch, *Dollars and Dictators: A Guide to Central America* (New York: Grove, 1983), 185.

20. *Latin America Weekly Report,* Weekly Report 32 (Aug. 17, 1984).

21. Lawyers Committee for International Human Rights and Americas Watch, *El Salvador's Other Victims: The War on the Displaced* (New York: Lawyers Committee for International Human Rights and Americas Watch, April 1984), 9.

22. U.S. Senate Committee on the Judiciary, Subcommittee on Immigration and Refugee Policy, *Refugee Problems in Central America* (Washington, D.C.: Government Printing Office, Sept. 1983), 2.

23. Angela Berryman, *Central American Refugees: A Survey of the Current Situation* (Philadelphia: American Friends Service Committee [hereafter AFSC], 1983), 3.

24. U.S. Senate, *Problems in Central America,* 12.

25. Frank Sharry, "Displaced persons: Humanitarian challenge in Central America," *World Refugee Survey 1984* (New York: U.S. Committee for Refugees, 1984), 26.

26. Lawyers Committee, *El Salvador's Other Victims,* 95.

27. Sam Dillon, "Second war in Salvador—Over refugees," Philadelphia *Inquirer* (Jan. 2, 1985), 3A.

28. See, for example, the Lawyers' Committee for International Human Rights, *El Salvador's Other Victims,* 16.

29. *Ibid.,* 50-80.

30. *Ibid.,* 126.

31. U.S. Senate, *Problems in Central America.*

32. Lawyers' Committee, *El Salvador's Other Victims,* 12.

33. U.S. Senate, *Problems in Central America,* 15.

34. Cited in James Y. Bradford, "Guatemala: A people besieged," AFSC Mimeo, 1978.

35. Amnesty International, "Memorandum presented to the government of the Republic of Guatemala, following a mission to the country from 10 to 15 August 1979" (London: Amnesty International, 1979).

36. *Central America Report* 5, No. 1 (February/March, 1985):5.

37. U.S. House and Senate, *Country Reports on Human Rights Practices for 1983* (Washington, D.C.: Government Printing Office, 1984), 577-91.

38. See Grupo de Apoyo a Refugiados Guatemaltecos, *Informe de Un Genocidio: Los Refugiados Guatemaltecos* (México: Ediciones La Paz, 1983).

39. Grupo de Apoyo a Refugiados Guatemaltecos, *El Refugiado* 3 (julio/agosto, 1983).

40. Lincoln, "Central America," 200.

41. *Latin America Weekly Report* (June 1, 1984).

42. Center for Research and Documentation of the Atlantic Coast (CIDCA), *Trabil Nani* (New York: Riverside Church Disarmament Program, 1984); Philippe Bourgois, "Nicaragua's ethnic minorities in the Revolution," *Monthly Review* 36, No. 8 (Jan. 1985), 22-44.

43. These figures and the summary of the historical development of the indigenous groups are largely drawn from Bourgois, "Nicaragua's Ethnic Minorities," 22-44, and CIDCA, *Trabil Nani.* As in most studies, the indigenous groups are referred to as

"Miskitus", as the Miskitus represent the largest group within Nicaragua's ethnic minorities.

44. Mark Malloch Brown, "Nicaraguan Miskitos," *Refugees,* 1 (Sept. 1982), 17.

45. Cited in CIDCA, *Trabil Nani,* 7.

46. Roxanne (Dunbar) Ortiz, "Miskitus in Nicaragua: Who is violating human rights?" in Stanford California Action Network, ed. *Central America in Revolution* (Boulder, CO: Westview, 1983), 466-70.

47. Bourgois, "Nicaragua's ethnic minorities," 28.

48. *Ibid.*

49. Robert L. Solomon, *The Politics of Exile: Views of the Guatemalan Experience,* Rand Corporation Study, 1968.

50. "Asylum in Mexico," *Refugees Magazine* 1 (Sept. 1982), 24.

51. Thomas Walsh, "Refugee crisis heightens," *Central American Report* 3, No. 2 (1983), 3.

CHAPTER 3

1. For a more complete discussion of Mexico's policies toward the refugees, particularly with respect to bureaucratic conflicts over refugee policy, see Elizabeth G. Ferris, "The politics of asylum: Mexico and the Central American refugees," *J. InterAmerican Studies and World Affairs* 26, No. 3 (Aug. 1984), 357-84.

2. Julio Hernández and René Delgado, "No debe cederse ante provoácaciones come la de Guatemala: la comisión permanente," *Uno más uno* (3 de febrero 1983), 4.

3. Jorge Eduardo Rodriguez, "Fin a deportaciones masivas; asilo político selectivo," *Proceso* 244 (6 de julio 1981), 24.

4. There are many excellent studies of politics in Mexico. See Kenneth F. Johnson, *Mexican Democracy: A Critical View* (New York: Praeger, 1978) and L. V. Padgett, *The Mexican Political System,* 2nd ed. (Boston: Houghton Mifflin, 1976). Daniel Levy and Gabriel Szekely, *Mexico: Paradoxes of Stability and Change* (Boulder, CO: Westview, 1983) is a good summary discussion of current Mexican political institutions and processes. The recently published, *International Inventory of Current Mexico-Related Research,* edited and published by the Center for U.S.-Mexican Studies at the University of California, San Diego (1984), is a good source for current research on the Mexican political system.

5. Maria Luisa Cabral, "El ACNUR, La asistencia internacional a los refugiados," *Relaciones Internacionales* IV, No. 12 (1976), 33-48.

6. Personal interviews, Mexico, 1983.

7. There are many excellent studies of U.S.-Mexican relations. See George W. Grayson, *The United States and Mexico* (New York: Praeger, 1984) for a good overview of the issues. *Mexican-U.S. Relations: Conflict and Convergence,* edited by Carlos Vásquez and Manuel García y Griego (Los Angeles: UCLA Chicano Studies Research Center Publications and UCLA Latin American Center Publication, 1983) is an excellent collection of articles on U.S.-Mexican relations.

8. Octavio Paz and Carlos Fuentes are probably the best-known Mexican authors who have explored these ideals. See, for example, *El laberinto de la soledad* (Mexico: Fondo de Cultura Economica, 1959) and *El arco y la lira* (Mexico: Fondo de Cultura Economica, 1972), by Paz, and Carlos Fuentes' *Terra Nostra* (Mexico: Joaquin Mortiz, 1975).

9. For a more complete discussion of these contradictions, see Elizabeth G. Ferris, "Mexico's foreign policies: A study in contradictions," in *The Dynamics of Latin American Foreign Policies: Challenges for the 1980s,* Jennie K. Lincoln and Elizabeth G. Ferris, eds. (Boulder, CO: Westview, 1984), 213-28. Also see, "Mexican policy toward Central America and the Caribbean" in *Revolution and Counterrevolution in Central America and the Carribean,* Donald E. Schulz and Douglas H. Graham, eds. (Boulder, CO: Westview, 1984), 423-46; and Edward J. Williams, "Mexico's Central

American policy: Revolutionary and prudential dimensions," in *The Colossus Challenged: The Struggle for Caribbean Influence*, H. Michael Erisman and John D. Martz, eds. (Boulder, CO: Westview, 1982), 149-70.

10. Olga Pellicer, "Mexico in Central America: The difficult exercise of regional power," in Richard R. Fagen and Olga Pellicer, eds. *The Future of Central America: Policy Choices for the U.S. and Mexico* (Stanford, CA: Stanford Univ. Press, 1983), 120.

11. *Ibid.*, 121.

12. *Latin American Regional Reports* (Nov. 20, 1980).

13. *Latin America Weekly Report* (June 15, 1984); Leslie Gelb, "Mexico cooling on Latin rebels, U.S. officials say" New York *Times* (July 19, 1984), 1A.

14. Adolfo Aguilar Zinser, "Mi desacuerdo con la política exterior," *Suplemento político de Uno más uno* (29 de julio 1984).

15. Aguilar, "Mexico and the Guatemalan Crisis," 169.

16. Aguilar, "Mi desacuerdo," 169.

17. *Dollars and Sense* (July/Aug. 1983), 7.

18. *Latin America Weekly Report* (Jan. 27, 1984).

19. *Wall Street Journal* (May 2, 1984).

20. *Latin America Weekly Report* (April 6, 1984); *Latin America Regional Report* (March 23, 1984).

21. Julie Brill, "Guatemalan refugees: Will Mexico's 'welcome' last?" *The Nation* 238, No. 19 (May 19, 1984), 603.

22. American Civil Liberties Union, National Immigration and Alien Rights Project, *Salvadorans in the United States: The Case for Extended Voluntary Departure*, Report No. 1 (Washington, D.C.: ACLU, 1983), A29-A31.

23. Coordinadora de Ayuda a Refugiados Guatemaltecos, *Boletín Informativo* 2 (marzo 1983); Grupo de Apoyo a Refugiados Guatemaltecos (GARS), *La Contrainsurgencia y los Refugiados Guatemaltecos* (México: Federación Editorial Mexicana, 1983), and *Informe de un Genocidio.*

24. *Latin America Regional Reports* (April 30, 1982), 8.

25. Jeremy Adelman, "Guatemalan refugees in Mexico," *Refuge* 3, No. 2 (1983), 7, 10-11; *El Refugiado* (julio/agosto 1983), 4.

26. U.S. General Accounting Office, *Central American Refugees: Regional Conditions and Potential Impact on the United States* (GAO NSIAD-84-106) (Washington: GAO, 1984), 25, 28. For reports on the general situation of the refugees, see ACLU, *Salvadorans in the U.S.*, A29-A30; and GARG, *La Contrainsurgencia.*

27. Ricardo del Muro, David Siller, and Miguel Angel Velazquez, "Hay en Mexico 231 mil immigrantes de 81 países," *Uno más Uno* (22 de julio 1982), 1, 6; and Kenneth F. Johnson and Miles W. Williams, *Illegal Aliens in the Western Hemisphere: Political and Economic Factors* (New York: Praeger, 1981), 8.

28. GARG, *La Contrainsurgencia.*

29. Federico Reyes Heroles, "Deportación de Guatemaltecos" *Uno más Uno* (21 de octobre, 1982), 1, 12.

30. Penny Lernoux, "Guatemalan army targets exiles," *National Catholic Reporter* 18 (May 21, 1982), 5.

31. ACLU, *Salvadorans in the U.S.*, A29-A31.

32. New York *Times* (June 22, 1983), 2.

33. *Ibid.*

34. Diana Torres, "Intervención en la mesa Redonda sobre 'corriente migratoria centroamericana a Mexico' Organizada por la Tribuna de Juventud," speech in Tuxtla Gutierrez, Mexico (mimeo, 1982), 12-15.

35. M. Buendia, "Red privada, 4" *Excelsior* (22 de enero 1982), 1.

36. R. Von Arnim, "Gira por la provincia de Chiapas," *Refugiados* (noviembre 1983), 17-18.

CHAPTER 4

1. On Costa Rican democracy generally, see Charles D. Ameringer, *Democracy in Costa Rica* (New York: Praeger 1982). Also see Charles Denton, "Costa Rica: a democratic revolution" in Howard J. Wiarda and Harvey F. Kline, eds. *Latin American Politics and Development* (Boston: Houghton Mifflin, 1979).

2. Barry et al., *Dollars and Dictators*, 198.

3. Ameringer, *Democracy in Costa Rica*, 94.

4. Joanne Kenen, "Costa Rica: practically neutral," *Atlantic Monthly* (March 1984), 31.

5. Jennie K. Lincoln, "Neutrality Costa Rican-style" (Mimeo 1985), 7.

6. Kenen, "Costa Rica," 34.

7. Robert D. Tomasek, "The deterioration of relations between Costa Rica and the Sandinistas," Center for Hemispheric Studies, America Enterprise Institute Occasional Papers, Series No. 9 (Sept. 1984), 4. Tomasek notes in footnote 4 that the actions of the Costa Rican government vis à vis Nicaragua are definitely supported by the population. A random poll in May 1983 in a Costa Rican newspaper found that 76 percent of the Costa Rican population approved of the way President Monge carried out relations with Nicaragua, and most Costa Ricans blamed Nicaragua for the deterioration in relations.

8. *Ibid.*

9. *Ibid.*, 13.

10. Cited by Lincoln, "Central America," 205.

11. *Latin America Weekly Report* (May 6, 1983).

12. Cited by Tomasek, "The Deterioration of Relations," 29.

13. *Washington Report on the Hemisphere*, 4, No. 11 (1982), 5.

14. Lincoln, "Neutrality," 2-3.

15. *Ibid.*

16. *Latin America Weekly Report* (Sept. 23, 1983).

17. *Latin America Weekly Report* (Nov. 18, 1983).

18. *Latin America Weekly Report* (Nov. 25, 1983).

19. Marc Edelman and Jayne Hutchcroft, "Costa Rica: Resisting authority," *NACLA* 18, No. 1 (Jan./Feb. 1984), 11.

20. Lincoln, "Central America," 207-08.

21. Lincoln, "Neutrality," 7.

22. Philip Berryman, "Yearning for peace in a widening war," *Friends Journal* (August 1/15, 1983), 12.

23. Claudio Gonzalez-Vega, "Fear of adjusting: The social costs of economic policies in Costa Rica in the 1970s," in Donald E. Schulz and Douglas H. Graham, eds. *Revolution and Counterrevolution in Central America and the Caribbean* (Boulder, CO: Westview, 1984), 353.

24. Kenen, "Costa Rica," 31.

25. Barry, et al. *Dollars and Dictators*, 203.

26. Gonzalez-Vega, "Fear of Adjusting," 355.

27. *Latin America Weekly Report* (Nov. 27, 1981; Dec. 3, 1982; Jan. 29, 1982).

28. *Latin America Weekly Report* (Oct. 15, 1982).

29. *Washington Report on the Hemisphere* 3, No. 22 (Aug. 23, 1983).

30. *Latin America Regional Report* (Sept. 23, 1982).

31. Lincoln, "Neutrality," 15; and *Latin America Weekly Report* (Sept. 30, 1983).

32. Berryman, "Yearning for Peace," 9; and *Latin America Weekly Report* (June 29, 1984).

33. Lincoln, "Neutrality," 13.

34. Colon Bermúdez, "Durable solutions in Costa Rica," *Refugees* 1 (Sept. 1982), 18.

35. U.S. GAO, *Central American Refugees,* 20. These figures were continually given to the author in interviews with governmental and nongovernmental officials in Costa Rica.

36. Bermúdez, "Durable Solutions," 18.

37. Personal interviews with the author in March 1984 in San José, Costa Rica. Other direct quotes of Costa Rican officials in this chapter are taken from interviews conducted at the same time.

38. Marlene Cambronero, "Refugiados en Costa Rica, 15 mil almas buscan libertad," *La Nacion International* (28 de julio/3 de agosto, 1983), 15.

CHAPTER 5

1. Cited by Walter LaFeber, *Inevitable Revolutions: The United States in Central America* (New York: W. W. Norton and Co., 1984), 124.

2. James A. Morris, "Honduras: A unique case," in Howard J. Wiarda and Harvey F. Kline, eds. *Latin American Politics and Development* (Boston: Houghton Mifflin Co., 1979). 347.

3. Steven Volk, "Honduras: On the border of the war" *NACLA Report on the Americas,* XV, No. 6 (Nov./Dec. 1981), 6.

4. *Ibid.*, 8. Note too the similarities with the 1984 situation in Costa Rica when a "successful" strike was followed by a company decision to pull out of the country.

5. LaFeber, *Inevitable Revolutions,* 182.

6. By 1968 U.S. multinational corporations controlled 100 percent of the production of Honduras' five largest firms, 88.7 percent of the 20 largest, and 82 percent of the 50 largest (Volk, "Honduras," 6).

7. Barry, et al., *Dollars and Dictators,* 165.

8. Mark B. Rosenberg, "Honduras: Bastion of stability or quagmire?" in Schulz and Graham, eds. *Revolution and Counterrevolution,* 334.

9. *Latin America Weekly Report,* April 6, 1984; Eva Gold, "High stakes," *Sojourners Magazine* (Aug. 1984); Eva Gold, "Honduras: The U.S. military buildup and human rights" (Philadelphia: NARMIC, 1984).

10. Rosenberg, "Honduras: Bastion of stability or quagmire?" 342.

11. Mark B. Rosenberg, "Nicaragua and Honduras: Toward garrison states," *Current History* 83, No. 490 (Feb. 1984), 59.

12. Barry et al., *Dollars and Dictators,* 163.

13. Tom Harden, "Honduras: Pushed over the edge," *Fellowship* 50, No. 6 (June 1984), 11.

14. Gold, "Honduras: The U.S. military buildup."

15. *Latin America Weekly Report* (Aug. 31, 1984).

16. "Update Central America," (Sept. 1984), 1.

17. Barry et al., *Dollars and Dictators,* 160.

18. *Ibid.*, 167.

19. *Latin America Regional Report,* (Aug. 17, 1984).

20. Rosenberg, "Nicaragua and Honduras," 60; "Honduras: A democracy in demise," *WOLA Update* (Feb. 1984), 3.

21. *Latin America Weekly Report* (July 13, 1984).

22. Lawyer's Committee for International Human Rights, *Honduras: On the Brink* (New York: Lawyers Committee for International Human Rights 1984). UNHCR Fact Sheets on Central America were used for reporting of numbers of refugees in Honduras.

23. Jeremy Adelman, "The insecurity of the El Salvadoran refugees," *Refuge* 3(1), 1, 3, 4.

24. David Blundy, "Victims of the massacre that the world ignored," in Stanford Central America Action Network, ed. *Revolution in Central America* (Boulder, CO: Westview, 1983), 337-42; Yvonne Dilling, with Ingrid Rogers, *In Search of Refuge* (Scottsdale, PA: Herald Press, 1984).

25. Leyda M. Barbieri, "Honduras: the Church, the Army and the Refugees," *New Catholic World* 224 (Sept./Oct. 1981), 231.

26. For a personal account of the activities of these protection officers, see Nicholas Van Praag, "A short walk along the border," *Refugees,* 15 (March 1985), 17-18.

27. Philip E. Wheaton, *Inside Honduras* (Washington, D.C.: Epica Task Force 1982), 14.

28. Adrian Penniak and Steve Askin, "Refugees tell of abuse at hands of agency," *National Catholic Reporter* 18 (April 23, 1982), 35.

29. Wheaton, *Inside Honduras,* 33.

30. Dilling and Rogers, *In Search of Refuge.*

31. David J. Kalke, "Central America's refugees: A litany of suffering," *Christian Century* (Nov. 10, 1982), 1138.

32. Thomas Walsh, "Refugees face new threat," *Central American Report* 3, No. 2 (1983), 8.

33. Martin Barber and Meyer Brownstone, "Relocating refugees in Honduras," *Refuge* 3, No. 2 (Dec. 1983), 12-15.; Dilling and Rogers, *In Search of Refuge.*

34. Alma Guillermoprieta, "Salvadoran refugees resist Honduras' plan to move them," Washington *Post* (March 22, 1984), A29. See also Lawyers Committee, *Honduras on the Brink,* and U.S. GAO, *Central American Refugees.*

35. Mary Solberg, "Reflections on a tour," *Christianity and Crisis* 42 (Nov. 29, 1982), 386.

36. Richard Day and Jerry Tinker, "Staff report for the use of the Subcommittee on Immigration and Refugee Policy, Judiciary Committee," Mimeo (Sept. 21, 1983), 8.

37. ACLU, *Salvadorans in the U.S.,* 45.

38. Guillermoprieta, "Salvadoran refugees," A29.

39. Larry Cohen, "One more river to cross," *Christianity and Crisis* (Nov. 29, 1982), 389.

40. U.S. GAO, *Central American Refugees* (pp. 17-19) describes the conflicts between the Honduran government and the UNHCR in deciding how these *ladino* relatives of the *contras* should be treated.

41. Florence Egal, "Imponer la esperanza en Mocorón," *Refugiados* (noviembre 1983), 9-11.

CHAPTER 6

1. Charles B. Keely, *U.S. Immigration: A Policy Analysis* (New York: Population Council, 1979), 8.

2. David M. Reimers, "Recent immigration policy: An analysis," in Barry R. Chiswick, ed. *The Gateway: U.S. Immigration Issues and Policies* (Washington, D.C.: American Enterprise Institute, 1982), 13.

3. Gallagher, "United States refugee policy," 18.

4. Reimers, *The Gateway,* 21, and Keely, *U.S. Immigration,* 35.

5. Michael S. Teitelbaum, "Right versus right: Immigration and refugee policy in the United States," *Foreign Affairs* 59, No. 1 (1980), 34.

6. Keely, *U.S. Immigration,* 69.

7. John A. Scanlan and G. D. Loescher, "Mass asylum and human rights in American foreign policy," *Political Science Quarterly* 97, No. 1 (1982), 39.

8. *Ibid.*

9. Cited by Victor H. Palmieri, "Foreword," in *U.S. Immigration and Refugee Policy: Global and Domestic Issues* (Lexington, MA: Lexington Books, 1983), xix.

10. Arnold H. Leibowitz, "The Refugee Act of 1980: Problems and Congressional concerns," *The Annals of the American Academy of Political and Social Science* 467 (May 1983), 167.

11. Robert Pear, "Cuban aliens, but not Haitians will be offered residency status," New York *Times* (Feb. 12, 1984), 1.

12. There are many excellent studies of U.S.-Central American relations, including LaFeber, *Inevitable Revolutions;* Richard Alan White, *The Morass: United States Intervention in Central America* (New York: Harper & Row, 1984); Martin Diskin, ed., *Trouble in Our Backyard* (New York: Pantheon Books, 1982); and Richard E. Feinberg, *Central America: International Dimensions of the Crisis* (New York: Holmes and Meier, 1982).

13. Barry et al., *Dollars and Dictators,* 40, 63.

14. Feinberg, *Central America: International Dimensions,* 75.

15. Wayne S. Smith, "Reagan's Central American policy: Disaster in the making," in Schulz and Graham, eds. *Revolution and Counterrevolution,* 486.

16. *Ibid.,* 487.

17. William M. LeoGrande, *Central America and the Polls* (Washington, D.C.: Washington Office on Latin America, 1984), 40.

18. Wayne A. Cornelius, "America in the era of limits: Migrants, nativists, and the future of U.S.-Mexican relations: Conflict and Convergence," in Carlos Vásquez and Manuel Garciá y Griego, eds. *Mexican-U.S. Relations: Conflict and Convergence* (Los Angeles: Univ. California Los Angeles, 1983), 385.

19. *Ibid.,* 387.

20. U.S. Committee for Refugees, "Public attitudes on refugees" (New York, mimeo, 1984).

21. ACLU, *Salvadorans in the U.S.;* Berryman, *Central American Refugees;* Juel Kamke, "500,000 Refugees in U.S.," *El Salvador Report* 1, No. 9 (Oct./Nov. 1981), 1, 7.

22. Personal interviews, January 1984.

23. Renny Golden and Michael McConnell, "Sanctuary: Choosing sides," *Christianity and Crisis,* 43, No. 2 (1983), 36.

24. ACLU, *Salvadorans in the U.S.,* 13.

25. Berryman, *Central American Refugees,* 6.

26. Gary MacEoin and Anita Riley, *No Promised Land: American Refugee Policies and the Rule of Law* (Boston: Oxfam, 1982), 41; Patrick A. Taran, "Refugees from El Salvador: In double jeopardy," *Church and Society* (Presbyterian Church) (Nov./Dec. 1981).

27. James Ridgeway, "El Norte: The road from Nicaragua," *VOICE* (June 19, 1984), 25-26.

28. David Quammen, "Knowing the heart of a stranger," *New Age Journal* (Aug. 1984), 33-40, 72; Renny Golden, "Sanctuary," *Sojourners* (Dec. 1982), 24-26; Golden and McConnell, *Christianity and Crisis,* 36; Martha Miller, "Mercy proclaimed in action," *The Catholic Worker* I, No. 1 (1983), 1.

29. Ronald Copeland and Patricia Weiss Fagen, "Political asylum: A background paper on concepts, procedures and problems" (Washington, D.C.: Refugee Policy Group, 1982), 19.

30. Kamke, "500,000 Refugees," 1, 7.

31. Austin, personal interview, January 1984.

32. Copeland and Fagen, "Political Asylum," 22.

33. Austin, personal interview, January 1984, and INS publications.

34. Personal interview, January 1984.

35. Michael Heilman, remarks presented at the Conference on Ethical Issues in U.S. Refugee Policy (Washington, D.C.: U.S. Coordinator for Refugee Affairs, 1983).

36. U.S. Coordinator for Refugee Affairs, *Conference on Ethical Issues in U.S. Refugee Policy,* edited transcript (Washington, D.C.: U.S. Coordinator for Refugee Affairs, March 1983):13.

37. Mary Thornton, "Refusing asylum to Salvadorans may violate pact, UN probe finds," Washington *Post* (Jan. 31, 1982), A17.

38. The sanctuary movement has been extensively covered in religious publications and in *Central America Report*. See, for example, Golden and McConnell, "Sanctuary: Choosing Sides," 31-36; Fred Drueger, "Land of the free, home of the eligible," *Christianity and Crisis* (July 9, 1984), 274-78; Quammen, "Knowing the Heart of a Stranger."

39. Don Oberdorfer, "Shultz hints at asylum for guerrillas," Washington *Post* (Aug. 8, 1983).

40. Taran, "Refugees from El Salvador."

41. Francis X. Clines, "Reagan says Salvadoran foes would bring U.S. refugees," *New York Times* (June 23, 1983).

42. Juan Williams, "White House pitches Latin policy to the public," Washington *Post* (Sept. 24, 1983), A5.

43. Norman L. Zucker, "Refugeê resettlement in the United States: Policy and problems," *Annals of the American Academy of Political and Social Science* 467 (May 1983), 181-82.

44. Wheaton, *Inside Honduras,* 34.

45. Gallagher, "United States refugee policy," 16.

46. Zucker, "Refugee resettlement," 82.

47. Cited in Nathaniel Sheppard, Jr., "Rights groups see bias in policies on refugees," *New York Times* (Aug. 5, 1983).

48. Michael H. Posner, "Asylum ajudication process," in Lydio F. Tomasi, ed. *In Defense of the Alien* 6 (New York: Center for Migration Studies), 96.

49. Michael S. Teitelbaum, "Immigration refugees and foreign policy," *International Organization* 38, No. 3 (Summer 1984), 429-50.

50. Personal interview, 1984.

51. Comments by Michael Teitelbaum in U.S. Coordinator for Refugee Affairs, *Conference on Ethical Issues in U.S. Refugee Policy.* (Washington: State Department, 1983), 17-21.

CHAPTER 7

1. Annick Billard, "Entrevista con Hussain Khan," *Refugiados* (noviembre 1983), 15.

2. Mitchell A. Seligson and William J. Carroll, III, "The Costa Rican role in the Sandinista victory," in Thomas W. Walker, ed. *Nicaragua in Revolution* (New York: Praeger, 1982), 331-44.

3. As Juan Tamayo ("Militants flock to Nicaragua," Philadelphia *Inquirer,* March 10, 1985) explains, revolutionaries from throughout Latin America have come to Managua to enjoy the relative freedom of movement that they find there. These individuals are not considered refugees.

4. Billard, *Refugiados,* 15-16; interview with Jose Mendiluce, "Priority to rural integration," *Refugees* 9 (Sept. 1984), 9-10; interview with Michel Moussali, *Refugees* 7 (July 1984), 9-10.

5. "The Dawson report," *Refuge* 2 (Dec. 1982).

6. U.S. Department of State, *Country Reports on the World Refugee Situation. Report to Congress for FY 1984* (Washington, D.C.: Department of State, 1983), 105.

7. Gerald E. Dirks, "Canada's policy towards the refugee phenomenon in Central America." Paper presented at the 1983 meeting of the International Studies Association, Mexico City.

8. *Ibid.,* 6.

9. David Matar, "Canada as a country of first asylum," *Refuge* 4, No. 2 (Dec. 1984); 22-24.

10. Colon Bermudez, "Guatemala: Christian Youth Association," *Refugees* 9 (Sept. 1984), 39-40.

11. John C. Everitt, "Small in numbers, but great in impact: The refugee migrations of Belize, Central America." Paper presented at the Symposium on Refugee Migrations in the Developing World, Manitoba, Canada (August 1983); Kofi Asomani, "Belize settlement project," *Refugees Magazine* 1 (Sept. 1982), 22; UNHCR, "Belize: River valley rural settlement," Mimeo (San José: UNHCR, 1984).

12. Clay, *World Refugee Survey 1984*, 13.

13. *Ibid.*, 14.

14. Hans-Joachim Hoffman-Nowotny, "Sociological approach toward a general theory of migration." in Mary M. Kritz, Charles B. Keely, and Silvano M. Tomasi, eds. *Global Trends in Migration* (New York: Center for Migration Studies, 1981), 64-83.

INDEX

About the Author

ELIZABETH G. FERRIS is Assistant Professor of Government and Law at Lafayette College in Easton, Pennsylvania. A specialist in Latin American foreign policies, she became interested in refugee issues while conducting research in Mexico as a Fulbright Professor. Since then she has interviewed governmental officials, refugees, and representatives of refugee-related private organizations in the United States, Mexico, Central America, and Geneva. Financial assistance was provided by the Heinz Endowment and by the Committee on Advanced Study and Research at Lafayette College. She has published extensively in the area of refugee studies and Latin American foreign policies in journals such as the *Journal of Inter-American Studies and World Affairs, International Organization,* and *The World Today.* She has edited or co-edited *Refugees in World Politics* (Praeger 1985), *The Dynamics of Latin American Foreign Policies* (Westview 1984), and *Latin American Foreign Policies: Global and Regional Dimensions* (Westview 1982). In 1985 she assumed the post of Refugee Secretary at the World Council of Churches in Geneva with responsibility for researching and writing on global refugee situations.